C O O L
Desserts

COOL
Desserts

J A N E   S U T H E R I N G
P H O T O G R A P H S   B Y   L I N D A   B U R G E S S

Meredith® Press
New York, New York

Published by
Meredith® Press
150 East 52nd Street
New York, NY 10022

©Salamander Books Ltd 1991
London

Editors: KRYSTYNA MAYER AND LISA DYER
Designer: PETER BRIDGEWATER
Photographer: LINDA BURGESS
Home Economist: JANE SUTHERING
Assistant Home Economist: MEG JANSZ
Stylist: DEBORAH PATTERSON
Illustrator: LORRAINE HARRISON
Color Reproduction: SCANTRANS PTE LTD.,
SINGAPORE

All correspondence should be addressed to
Meredith® Press.

ISBN: 0-696-02456-X

Distributed by Meredith Corporation
Des Moines, Iowa

This book may not be sold outside
the United States of America.

Printed in Singapore

C O N T E N T S

INTRODUCTION

This book is divided into five chapters containing many original ideas for making delicate custards, crisp meringues, creamy mousses, ice creams, sorbets and simple fruit desserts.

Whatever you choose to make, remember that the dessert is an important part of a meal and that it should be balanced with the other courses. If, for example, you have served a rich main course of red meat and a robust sauce, then the accompanying dessert should be light and refreshing, like a sorbet or a selection of fresh fruit. Conversely, a light main course of delicate fish may be partnered with a more substantial dessert such as a tart or gateau.

Another rule to remember is to avoid repetition of flavors and textures in a menu. For instance, do not use the same fruit in the main course and the dessert, and never serve more than one rich egg dish in a menu.

Color and appearance are important with all foods, but as the culminating point of a meal, desserts merit particularly exciting and attractive presentation. There is an enormous choice of serving dishes and decorations available and you should always consider these carefully before making your dessert. As the photographs in this book show, simple decorations like tiny fruit, leaves or swirls of piped cream enhance a dessert enormously. Suggestions for presentation are given with the recipes that follow, but you can adapt these at will to suit your preference.

CLOCKWISE FROM THE TOP, LEFT: *Chilled apples; Poached pears in spiced cider; Orchard fruit compote; Florentine zuccotto; Rose petal and strawberry ice cream; Pineapple and yogurt ice cream*

FROZEN ASSETS

This chapter contains a selection of delicious and unusual recipes for ice creams, sorbets and water ices, as well as many ideas for presentation.

Rich ice creams are made with egg yolks, sugar, heavy cream and added flavorings. Used in the right balance, these basic ingredients produce a firm ice cream that may be stored in the freezer for up to three months. These ice creams should always be softened before serving. This is best done in the refrigerator, although small quantities may be softened at room temperature.

Both sorbets and water ices are based on sugar syrup which is flavored and then frozen, often after the addition of whisked egg white to give a softer consistency. Like ice creams, they can be stored for up to three months. Most sorbets and water ices benefit from being softened a little before serving.

Several ice-cream machines are available that work on the principle of churning a prepared mixture in a chilled barrel until soft-frozen. Ice cream made in this way can either be served immediately or frozen in a container until required. If you intend making large amounts of frozen desserts, it is worthwhile investing in an ice-cream machine – the mixture can be frozen and ready to eat in 10–15 minutes.

If you do not own an ice-cream machine, you can still make ice cream. The simplest way to do this is to half-freeze a prepared mixture in a rigid container and then either beat it with a hand-held mixer or work it in a food processor until smooth to break down the ice crystals that form. The mixture can then be frozen until required. Extra beating during the freezing process makes the ice cream even smoother.

CONTENTS

WHITE CHOCOLATE ICE CREAM

SERVES 6 – 8

≈

....

5 ounces white chocolate
1¼ cups milk
¼ cup superfine sugar
1¼ cups heavy cream, lightly whipped

....

■ Break the chocolate into pieces, then place in a heat-proof bowl set over a saucepan of simmering water with the milk and sugar and heat until the chocolate has melted. Leave to cool, then fold in the lightly whipped cream and freeze in a rigid container until half-frozen. Beat until smooth. Alternatively, freeze in an ice-cream machine following the manufacturer's directions. Freeze again until required.

VARIATION

DOUBLE CHOCOLATE ICE CREAM

Substitute good-quality semisweet chocolate for the white chocolate in the above recipe. Use only ⅔ cup milk and 2 cups marshmallows. Melt these with the sugar in a saucepan over a very gentle heat. Follow the above recipe. Stir in 2 ounces finely chopped semisweet chocolate before the final freezing.

SERVING SUGGESTION: Serve scoops of the above ice creams together and decorate with chocolate leaves. To make chocolate leaves, melt a small amount of semisweet chocolate and brush it carefully on the underside of small rose leaves which have been washed and thoroughly wiped dry. Chill until firm, then repeat the process at least once more. Chill until the chocolate has set, then carefully peel off the rose leaves. Keep in a cool place. It is best to make these leaves on the day they are required as they tend to go white if stored.

TOFFEED WALNUT ICE CREAM

SERVES 6 – 8

≈

....

1 cup shelled walnuts
6 tbsp superfine sugar
2 tbsp water
2 tbsp unsalted butter
1¼ cups milk
1¼ cups heavy cream
4 egg yolks
2 tbsp soft brown sugar

....

■ Roast the walnuts in a preheated 400°F oven for 10 minutes. Dissolve the superfine sugar in the water over a gentle heat, then boil until rich caramel in color. Stir in the butter and walnuts and transfer to a lightly greased cookie sheet. Leave to go cold.

■ Pour the milk into the saucepan in which the caramel was cooked and heat gently until any leftover caramel has dissolved. Add the cream and bring just to a boil. Beat the egg yolks with the soft brown sugar until pale. Stir in the milk and transfer to a heatproof bowl set over a saucepan of simmering water. Cook until the mixture has thickened enough to coat the back of a wooden spoon – about 20 minutes. Alternatively, cook in a microwave oven on a medium-high setting for 6–7 minutes, stirring every 30 seconds until thickened. Strain and leave to cool.

■ Freeze in an ice-cream machine following the manufacturer's directions. Alternatively, freeze in a rigid container. When half-frozen, beat well until smooth and stir in the walnuts. Freeze again until required.

TOP *Toffeed walnut ice cream;*
BOTTOM *White chocolate and Double chocolate ice creams*

ROSE PETAL AND STRAWBERRY ICE CREAM

SERVES 8

≈

. . . .

4 egg yolks

½ cup superfine sugar

1¼ cups light cream

1 ounce heavily scented red or pink rose petals, rinsed

1½ cups chopped ripe strawberries

2 tbsp rosewater

1 tbsp lemon juice

1¼ cups heavy cream, lightly whipped

. . . .

■ Beat the egg yolks with the sugar until pale. Bring the light cream just to a boil and pour onto the eggs. Cook in a heatproof bowl set over a saucepan of simmering water until the custard has thickened, or cook in a microwave oven on a medium-high setting for about 3 minutes, stirring every 30 seconds until thickened. Pass through a fine strainer, then add the rose petals and leave to cool.

■ Add the strawberries, rosewater and lemon juice to the custard and puree in a blender. Fold in the whipped cream and freeze in a rigid container until half-frozen, then beat well and freeze again until required. Alternatively, freeze in an ice-cream machine according to the manufacturer's directions.

PINEAPPLE AND YOGURT ICE CREAM

SERVES 6

≈

The flavor of this ice cream is very much dependent on the ripeness of the pineapple. A ripe pineapple smells very sweet, the outside skin looks golden and the central leaves can be pulled off without any resistance.

. . . .

2 cups fresh pineapple puree

½ cup superfine sugar

1¼ cups yogurt

⅔ cup heavy cream, lightly whipped

. . . .

■ Cook the pineapple puree with the sugar over a medium heat for 5 minutes, stirring occasionally. Leave to go cold, then fold in the yogurt and cream. Freeze in a rigid container until half-frozen, then beat well and freeze again until required. Alternatively, freeze in an ice-cream machine following the manufacturer's directions.

Rose petal and strawberry ice cream and
Pineapple and yogurt ice cream

LEMON BALM ICE CREAM

SERVES 8

≈

This ice cream looks particularly pretty served in lemon shells. Choose even-sized, well-colored lemons. Cut a small amount off the bottom of each lemon so that it will stand straight. Slice a lid off the tops of the lemons and carefully scoop out the flesh. Freeze the shells until firm. Scoop or pipe the ice cream into the shells and replace the lids if desired. Freeze until required.

. . . .

small handful of lemon balm, washed
pared peel and juice of 1 lemon
1¼ cups milk
1¼ cups heavy cream
4 egg yolks
½ cup superfine sugar
frosted leaves (*page* 16), to decorate (optional)

. . . .

▨ Place the lemon balm, lemon peel, milk and cream in a saucepan and bring just to a boil. Remove from the heat and leave to infuse for about 1 hour, then strain through a fine strainer into a clean pan and reheat.
▨ Beat the egg yolks with the sugar until pale, then stir in the warm milk and cook in a heatproof bowl set over a saucepan of simmering water until the mixture just coats the back of a wooden spoon. Alternatively, cook in a microwave oven on a medium-high setting for 6–7 minutes, stirring every 30 seconds until thickened.
▨ Strain and leave to cool, then freeze in an ice-cream machine following the manufacturer's directions. Alternatively, freeze in a rigid container until half-frozen. Beat well until smooth and freeze again until required. The ice cream must be softened slightly if used to fill lemon shells. Decorate with frosted leaves, if desired.

VARIATION

TANGERINE ICE CREAM

Tangerines are ideally suited for grating and using as containers for ice cream. Omit the lemon balm and use the finely grated peel and juice of 2 tangerines in place of the lemon. Use only 6 tbsp superfine sugar. Follow the method for the recipe but do not strain the milk after it has been infused. If wished, fill hollowed-out tangerine shells with the ice cream as explained for lemons.

MANGO AND LIME SORBET

SERVES 4

≈

. . . .

2 firm, but ripe, mangoes, about 12 ounces each
½ cup granulated sugar
1 cup water
pared peel and juice of 2 limes
blanched lime julienne soaked in sugar syrup, to decorate (optional)

. . . .

▨ Wipe the mango skins, then score the fruit through the center with a sharp knife and twist the 2 halves of each mango apart. Catch any juice in a bowl. Carefully scoop out the flesh from each half and cut all the fruit from the seeds. Puree the fruit in a blender. Freeze the 4 half-skins.
▨ Place the sugar and water in a saucepan and dissolve over a gentle heat. Add the lime peel and bring to a boil. Bubble over medium heat for 5 minutes. Cool and strain, then add the mango puree and lime juice.
▨ Freeze in an ice-cream machine following the manufacturer's directions. Alternatively, freeze in a rigid container until half-frozen. Beat well and freeze again until quite firm. Spoon or pipe the sorbet into the mango skins, then freeze until required.
▨ If wished, the top of each sorbet can be decorated with a sprinkling of blanched lime julienne soaked in sugar syrup.

CLOCKWISE FROM THE TOP,
LEFT: *Lemon balm ice cream;*
Grapefruit water ice (recipe, page 16);
Tangerine ice cream; Mango and
lime sorbet

ORANGE WATER ICE

SERVES 8

≈

If wished, this water ice can be served in scooped-out orange skins (see page 14) and decorated with frosted bay leaves. To frost the leaves, brush them with egg white and dust with superfine sugar, then leave in a warm place to dry.

¾ cup granulated sugar
1½ cups water
1½ cups freshly squeezed orange juice
3 tbsp fresh lemon juice

■ Dissolve the sugar in the water over a gentle heat. Bring to a boil and boil for 5 minutes. Remove from the heat and add the orange and lemon juices. Freeze in an ice-cream machine following the manufacturer's directions. Alternatively, freeze in a rigid container until half-frozen. Beat well and freeze again until required.

VARIATION

GRAPEFRUIT WATER ICE

Use the slightly sweeter pink grapefruit when available. Simply replace the orange juice with grapefruit juice. You will need 3–4 grapefruit to make 1½ cups juice. To serve the water ice in the grapefruit skins, cut the grapefruit in half and scoop out the flesh and membrane. Using scissors, scallop the edge of each half-skin and cut a slice from the bottom of each so it will stand up straight. For the most decorative effect, pipe the lightly softened water ice into the shells using a pastry bag fitted with a large star tip. Freeze until required. Decorate the water ice with a sprig of mint just before serving.
(See picture, page 15.)

NECTARINE SORBET

SERVES 4 – 6

≈

1 pound ripe nectarines
1½ cups sorbet syrup (*see page 30*)
2 tbsp lemon juice
2 tbsp orange juice

■ Place the nectarines in a large bowl and just cover with boiling water. Leave for 10 seconds, then drain and cover with cold water. Drain and carefully remove the skins. Halve and pit the fruit, then chop roughly. Combine all the ingredients in a saucepan and bring to a boil. Leave to cool, then puree in a blender. Freeze in an ice-cream machine following the manufacturer's directions. Alternatively, freeze in a rigid container until half-frozen, then beat well and freeze again until required. Serve the sorbet in scoops, in an ice bowl (*see below*), if desired.

TO MAKE AN ICE BOWL

Choose two freezerproof glass bowls, one of about 7½-cup capacity and the other about 2½ cups. Choose a color scheme relevant to the ice creams or sorbets to be presented (in this case, marigold petals and sliced kumquats have been used for their bright orange color). Make layers of whole edible flowerheads, petals, sliced fruit and leaves of your choice mixed with crushed ice cubes and a little water in the large bowl. Freeze until solid after each layer has been completed (about 1 hour for each layer). After the first one or two layers have been made, position the smaller bowl in the center of the large bowl and weight it down so that it will not move as the new layers are started. Freeze the ice bowl, then unmold, wrap in plastic wrap and keep in the freezer until required.

Orange water ice and Nectarine sorbet
in an ice bowl.

ROSEMARY AND LEMON SORBET

SERVES 6 – 8

≈

. . . .

4 4-inch sprigs fresh rosemary

2½ cups boiling water

½ cup granulated sugar

⅔ cup cold water

pared peel of I lemon

I tbsp lemon juice

poached apple slices or

a selection of summer berries, to decorate

(optional)

. . . .

▧ Cover the rosemary sprigs with the boiling water and leave to infuse for 20 minutes, then strain through a fine strainer or cheesecloth. Place the sugar and remaining water in a saucepan and dissolve over a gentle heat. Add the lemon peel and bring to a boil. Bubble over a medium heat for 5 minutes, then strain and add to the rosemary water. Stir in the lemon juice.
▧ Freeze in a rigid container until half-frozen, then beat well and freeze again until required. Alternatively, freeze in an ice-cream machine following the manufacturer's directions.
▧ Soften the sorbet slightly. Using a pastry bag fitted with a large star tip, pipe the sorbet into glasses. Serve with poached apple slices or summer berries.

GOOSEBERRY AND ELDER FLOWER SORBET

SERVES 6 – 8

≈

Pureed gooseberries and freshly picked elder flower heads give this sorbet a wonderfully subtle flavor. Wild elder flowers are available in summer when their white flowers bloom. Never wash elder flowers before use because this reduces their natural fragrance. If elder flowers are unavailable, substitute 3 tbsp China tea, but infuse for only 20 minutes. A few drops of green food coloring may be added to the mixture before freezing.

. . . .

12 freshly picked elder flower heads

2½ cups boiling water

½ cup granulated sugar

⅔ cup cold water

6 ounces gooseberries

I tbsp lemon juice

elder flower blossoms, to decorate (optional)

. . . .

▧ Cover the elder flower heads with the boiling water and leave to infuse for I hour, then strain through a fine strainer or cheesecloth. Place the sugar and remaining water in a saucepan and dissolve over a gentle heat. Add the gooseberries and bring to a boil. Bubble over a medium heat for 5 minutes, then cool and puree in a blender. If wished, pass the puree through a fine strainer to remove the seeds.
▧ Add the elder flower water and lemon juice and freeze in an ice-cream machine following the manufacturer's directions. Alternatively, freeze in a rigid container until half-frozen. Beat well and freeze until required.
▧ Soften the sorbet slightly. Using a pastry bag fitted with a large star tip, pipe the sorbet into glasses. Sprinkle with elder flower blossoms, if desired.

LEFT *Rosemary and lemon sorbet;*
RIGHT *Gooseberry and elder flower sorbet*

CHERRY BOMBE

S E R V E S   6 – 8

≈

Special bombe molds are available, but a freezerproof bowl will do just as well for this recipe.

. . . .

ICE CREAM

4 egg yolks

¼ cup superfine sugar

2½ cups milk

⅔ cup heavy cream, lightly whipped

½ cup cherry brandy

SORBET

scant 1 cup water

6 tbsp granulated sugar

juice of ½ lemon

1½ cups pitted and roughly chopped cherries

2 tbsp kirsch

cookies, to serve

. . . .

▓ To make the ice cream, beat the egg yolks with the sugar until pale. Bring the milk just to a boil and add to the eggs. Stir well and cook in a heatproof bowl set over a saucepan of simmering water until the custard has thickened enough to coat the back of a wooden spoon. Alternatively, cook the custard in a microwave oven on a medium-high setting for 6–7 minutes, stirring every 30 seconds until thickened.

▓ Pass through a fine strainer, then leave to cool. Fold in the whipped cream and cherry brandy and freeze in a rigid container until half-frozen, then beat well until smooth. Alternatively, freeze in an ice-cream machine according to the manufacturer's directions.

▓ Spoon about seven-eighths of the ice cream into a chilled 5-cup bombe mold and press a 1¼-cup freezer-proof tumbler into the center to force the ice cream to the top of the mold at the sides. Leave the tumbler in place and freeze until solid. Keep the remaining ice cream frozen as this will be used later to make the bottom of the bombe. Remove the tumbler and smooth

the sides of the ice cream. Return to the freezer until required.

▓ To make the sorbet, place the water, sugar and lemon juice in a saucepan and heat gently until the sugar dissolves. Bring to a boil and boil for 5 minutes. Add the cherries and boil for a further 5 minutes. Leave to cool and stir in the kirsch. Freeze in a rigid container until half-frozen, then beat well and freeze until firm, or freeze in an ice-cream machine according to the manufacturer's directions.

▓ Fill the center of the bombe with the sorbet. Top with the reserved ice cream, so that the sorbet is enclosed. Freeze for at least 8 hours or until required.

▓ To unmold the bombe, place the mold on a plate and wrap a hot towel around it to loosen the ice cream. Remove the mold, then smooth the surface of the dessert with a spatula to neaten it. Freeze until just firm.

▓ Serve in wedges with cookies.

V A R I A T I O N S

Bombes can be made in many different flavors by altering the liqueur used in the ice cream and the fruit used in the sorbet. Try using Crème de Framboise with raspberries, Crème de Cassis with black currants, and Crème de Fraise with strawberries. If making a raspberry- or strawberry-flavored bombe, omit the kirsch from the sorbet and use brandy instead.

Cherry bombe

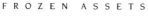

NESSELRODE DESSERT

SERVES 10

≈

....

⅓ cup dried currants or raisins

⅓ cup golden raisins

⅓ cup finely chopped candied peel

⅓ cup chopped candied or maraschino
cherries

⅓ cup chopped marron glacé (candied
chestnuts)

4 tbsp dark rum

4 egg yolks

1½ cups confectioners' sugar, sifted

2½ cups heavy cream

½ cup unsweetened chestnut puree

cookies, to serve

....

▦ Cover the currants, golden raisins and peel with boiling water and leave for 15 minutes to plump. Drain, then mix with the cherries and marron glacé. Add the rum and leave to marinate for at least 1 hour.

▦ Beat together the egg yolks and sugar until pale. Bring half the cream just to a boil and stir into the eggs. Cook in a heatproof bowl set over a saucepan of simmering water until the custard has thickened enough to coat the back of a wooden spoon. Alternatively, cook in a microwave oven on a medium-high setting for about 3 minutes, stirring every 30 seconds until thickened.

▦ Add a little custard to the chestnut puree and beat until smooth, then add the remaining custard. Leave to cool. Lightly whip the remaining cream and fold into the custard.

▦ Freeze in an ice-cream machine following the manufacturer's directions. Alternatively, freeze in a rigid container until half-frozen. Beat well and fold in the fruit and rum until evenly combined. Transfer the mixture to a 6¼-cup mold and freeze until required.

▦ Unmold and serve with cookies.

ROCKY ROAD ICE CREAM

SERVES 6 – 8

≈

This delicious and unusual ice cream gets its name from its very chunky texture.

....

4 egg yolks

½ cup superfine sugar

2½ cups milk

⅔ cup heavy cream, lightly whipped

4 ounces semisweet chocolate,
coarsely chopped

⅓ cup roasted, skinned peanuts

1 cup quartered marshmallows

cookies, to serve

....

▦ Beat the egg yolks with the sugar until pale. Bring the milk just to a boil and add to the eggs. Stir well and cook in a heatproof bowl set over a saucepan of simmering water until the custard has thickened enough to coat the back of a wooden spoon. Alternatively, cook the custard in a microwave oven on a medium-high setting for 6–7 minutes, stirring every 30 seconds until thickened. Pass through a fine strainer and leave to cool.

▦ Fold in the whipped cream and freeze in a rigid container until half-frozen, then beat well until smooth. Alternatively, freeze in an ice-cream machine following the manufacturer's directions. Stir in the remaining ingredients and freeze again until required.

▦ Serve with cookies.

TOP *Rocky road ice cream;*
BOTTOM *Nesselrode dessert*

CHRISTMAS ICE-CREAM MOLD

SERVES 10–12

≈

....

4 egg yolks

½ cup superfine sugar

2½ cups milk

⅔ cup heavy cream, lightly whipped

I cup grated eating apple

2 tbsp unsalted butter

⅓ cup dried currants

⅓ cup golden raisins

⅓ cup raisins

⅓ cup finely chopped candied orange peel

¼ cup soft brown sugar

¼ tsp ground cinnamon

¼ tsp ground nutmeg

¼ tsp apple pie spice

finely grated peel and juice of ½ lemon

finely grated peel and juice of ½ orange

¼ cup toasted and chopped walnuts

candied fruit, for decoration (optional)

....

▨ Beat the egg yolks with the sugar until pale. Bring the milk just to a boil, then pour onto the eggs and cook in a heatproof bowl set over a saucepan of simmering water until the custard has thickened. Alternatively, cook in a microwave oven on a medium-high setting for 6–7 minutes, stirring every 30 seconds until thickened. Pass through a fine strainer, then leave to cool. Fold in the whipped cream.

▨ Freeze in a rigid container until half-frozen, then beat well until smooth and return to the freezer until solid. Alternatively, freeze in an ice-cream machine following the manufacturer's directions.

▨ Sauté the apple in the butter until tender. Add all the remaining ingredients except the walnuts and simmer for about 5 minutes until the liquid has evaporated. Leave to cool, then stir in the walnuts.

▨ Soften the ice cream slightly, then beat well until smooth. Fold in the fruit mixture until evenly combined. Transfer to a 5½-cup freezerproof bowl. Cover and freeze for 6–8 hours or until required.

▨ Unmold and serve decorated with pieces of candied fruit, if desired.

PISTACHIO KULFI

SERVES 6

≈

A *quick version of a classic ice cream from India traditionally made with fresh milk which is reduced by boiling to a thick cream.*

....

20 green cardamom pods

1¾ cups evaporated milk

¼ cup superfine sugar

2 tsp unflavored gelatin

2 tbsp water

⅔ cup light cream

¼ cup skinned and finely chopped pistachio nuts

I tsp rosewater

pistachio nuts, to decorate (optional)

....

▨ Split the cardamom pods, being careful not to lose any of the seeds, and place them in a saucepan with the evaporated milk and sugar. Bring just to a boil, stirring until the sugar dissolves, then leave to infuse for I hour. Strain through a fine strainer. Dissolve the gelatin in the water over a gentle heat and stir into the milk with the remaining ingredients.

▨ Freeze in an ice-cream machine following the manufacturer's directions. Alternatively, freeze in a rigid container until half-frozen. Beat well and transfer the mixture to 6 dariole molds. Freeze until required.

▨ Unmold and serve on individual plates, decorated with pistachio nuts, if desired.

TOP *Christmas ice-cream mold;*
BOTTOM *Pistachio kulfi*

ON THE ROCKS

This chapter contains recipes for frozen desserts that are best served straight from the freezer, or that require freezing during some stage of the making process.

Since these desserts must be soft enough to be eaten straight from the freezer, sugar and alcohol, which retard freezing and therefore give softer consistencies, are important ingredients.

The simplest form of ice cream is known by its Italian name, semi-freddo, translated literally as "half-cold". The recipe consists of stiffly beating egg whites and then adding sugar, either in powder form or as a syrup, to give a thick, glossy meringue that can be flavored in numerous ways. Many of the recipes in this chapter are based on this principle.

Presentation is all-important. An attractive dessert will impress your guests and enhance any meal, therefore many of the following recipes are interestingly shaped, sometimes with contrasting layers, in loaf pans, cake pans and other molds. When unmolded, they can be topped with whipped cream and all types of fruit, nuts and other decorations of your choice.

C O N T E N T S

ICED RASPBERRY SOUFFLÉS

SERVES 6

≈

These desserts may be made well in advance and stored in the freezer with their paper collars in place to prevent any damage.

. . . .

2 cups raspberries
¾ cup plus 2 tbsp sugar
I tbsp lemon juice
½ cup water
4 egg whites
pinch of salt
I cup heavy cream, lightly whipped
fresh raspberries, to serve (optional)

. . . .

■ Wrap a collar of waxed paper around 6 individual ramekin dishes so that each collar comes about I inch above the top of the dish.
■ Puree the raspberries with 2 tbsp of the sugar and the lemon juice, then pass through a fine strainer to remove the seeds. Dissolve the remaining sugar in the water, then bring to a boil and boil until the temperature reaches 235°F on a candy thermometer. Beat the egg whites with a pinch of salt until stiff. As soon as the syrup reaches the correct temperature, beat it into the egg whites and continue beating until the mixture is cold.
■ Fold the raspberry puree and cream into the meringue mixture and divide between the ramekin dishes. Level the surface of each one and freeze for 4–6 hours until firm or until required. Carefully peel away the paper collars and serve with extra fresh rasp-berries, if desired.

ICED COCONUT MOUSSE

SERVES 6

≈

When fresh coconut is available, its grated flesh may be used instead of the shredded coconut. Strained coconut water can be used as part of the liquid content.

. . . .

½ cup shredded coconut
⅔ cup boiling water
¾ cup confectioners' sugar, sifted
I tbsp lime juice
2 tbsp Malibu (coconut liqueur)
¾ cup heavy cream, lightly whipped
2 egg whites
pinch of salt
fresh raspberries, to serve (optional)

. . . .

■ Mix together the coconut, water and half the sugar in a small saucepan. Boil for 3–4 minutes until the mixture has thickened and all the liquid has evaporated. Leave to cool, then stir in the lime juice and Malibu.
■ Fold in the whipped cream. Beat the egg whites with a pinch of salt until stiff, then beat in the remaining sugar a spoonful at a time. Fold into the coconut mixture and transfer to a 3¾-cup mold. Freeze for 6–8 hours until firm or until required.
■ Unmold and serve in slices with fresh raspberries, if desired, or any other fruit of your choice.

TOP *Iced raspberry soufflés;*
BOTTOM *Iced coconut mousse*

K I R   R O Y A L E   G R A N I T A

S E R V E S   6 - 8

≈

Kir Royale is a popular summer drink made up of champagne and Crème de Cassis (black currant liqueur) and this combination of flavors is equally good for a summer dessert.

. . . .

I cup black currants
1½ cups sorbet syrup *(see below)*
½ bottle champagne or dry sparkling white wine

. . . .

▩ Place the black currants and sorbet syrup in a saucepan and simmer for 5 minutes. Pass through a fine strainer and leave to cool. Stir in the champagne and freeze until the mixture forms flakes of ice. Stir well and serve in stemmed glasses.

S O R B E T   S Y R U P

M A K E S   6 ¼   C U P S

≈

. . . .

3⅓ cups superfine sugar
4½ cups water

. . . .

▩ Dissolve the sugar in the water over a gentle heat. Bring to a boil. Cool.

I C E D   P O R T   Z A B A G L I O N E

S E R V E S   6

≈

Decorate these desserts with fresh blackberries and sugar-frosted blackberry leaves. To frost the leaves, brush with a little egg white, then sprinkle with superfine sugar. Leave to dry in a warm place.

. . . .

6 egg yolks
6 tbsp superfine sugar
6 tbsp ruby port
I cup heavy cream
blackberries and frosted blackberry leaves, to decorate

. . . .

▩ Beat the egg yolks, sugar and port in a heatproof bowl set over simmering water for about 15 minutes until thick and foamy. Remove from the heat and continue beating until cold. Whip the cream until it just holds its shape, then fold into the egg mixture. Transfer to individual dishes and freeze for about 6 hours until firm or until required.
▩ Decorate with blackberries and frosted leaves just before serving.

V A R I A T I O N S

Sherry may be used as an alternative to the ruby port in this recipe. The Zabaglione can also be frozen and served in scooped-out lemon or orange shells. The flavor of the fruit will permeate through the dessert as it freezes. For the best results, use lemon shells if the Zabaglione includes ruby port and orange shells if made with sherry. Eight large lemons or 6 large oranges will be required for the amount of mixture in this recipe. Just before serving, top each dessert with an edible green leaf such as bay or lemon.

LEFT *Kir Royale granita;*
RIGHT *Iced port zabaglione*

STRAWBERRY-CREAM MERINGUE CAKE

SERVES 12-14

≈

A *delightful combination of strawberries, cream and meringue makes this a very special dessert ideal for a party. The meringue may be made well in advance and stored in airtight containers. Buy summer-ripe strawberries when they are at their least expensive, and make the ice cream or simply freeze the puree until required.*

. . . .

STRAWBERRY LAYERS

¾ pound ripe strawberries, hulled

heaped ¾ cup superfine sugar

I tbsp lemon juice

⅔ cup water

4 egg whites

pinch of salt

I cup heavy cream, lightly whipped

MERINGUE LAYERS

4 egg whites

pinch of salt

heaped I cup superfine sugar

TO ASSEMBLE

2½ cups heavy cream, whipped

cultivated and wild strawberries, with leaves
and flowers, to decorate

. . . .

▨ To make the strawberry layers, puree the strawberries with 2 tbsp of the sugar and the lemon juice. Dissolve the remaining sugar in the water, then bring to a boil and boil until the temperature reaches 235°F on a candy thermometer. Beat the egg whites with a pinch of salt until stiff. As soon as the syrup reaches the correct temperature, beat it into the egg whites and continue beating until the mixture is cold.

▨ Fold the strawberry puree and cream into the meringue mixture and divide between two 8-inch cake pans. Freeze for 4–6 hours until solid.

▨ To make the meringue layers, draw three 8-inch circles on 3 pieces of foil and place on 3 cookie sheets. Preheat the oven to 250°F.

▨ Beat the egg whites with a pinch of salt until stiff, then beat in the sugar a spoonful at a time until the mixture is thick and glossy. Fit a pastry bag with a large star tip and pipe 3 circles of meringue onto the pieces of foil, following the outlines. Use the spare meringue to pipe 16 rosettes. Bake the meringue circles and rosettes for 1 hour until crisp. Leave to go cold, then carefully peel off the foil.

▨ To assemble the cake, unmold the strawberry ice creams. Place a meringue circle on a large serving plate and spread a thin layer of cream on top. Place a round of ice cream on top and cover with a thin layer of cream. Repeat the layering, finishing with the last meringue circle.

▨ Sandwich the rosettes of meringue together with a little cream and arrange on top of the cake. Pipe rosettes of cream on the sides of the ice cream and decorate with small, halved strawberries. Arrange a few strawberries with leaves and flowers decoratively in the center of the cake.

Strawberry-cream meringue cake

INDIVIDUAL PEAR ALASKAS

SERVES 8

≈

....

ICE CREAM

2⅔ cups peeled, cored and diced pears

½ cup superfine sugar

2 tbsp lemon juice

2 egg yolks

⅔ cup light cream

⅔ cup heavy cream, lightly whipped

MERINGUE

4 egg whites

pinch of salt

½ cup superfine sugar

8 slices jelly roll

8 pear leaves, to decorate

....

▧ Combine the pears, half the sugar and the lemon juice and leave to one side.

▧ Beat the egg yolks with the remaining sugar until thick and pale. Bring the light cream just to a boil and stir into the eggs. Cook in a heatproof bowl set over a saucepan of simmering water until the mixture has thickened enough to coat the back of a wooden spoon. Alternatively, cook in a microwave oven on a medium-high setting for 2–3 minutes, stirring every 30 seconds until thickened. Pass through a fine strainer and leave to cool.

▧ Add the pear mixture to the custard and puree in a blender. Fold in the whipped cream.

▧ Freeze in an ice-cream machine following the manufacturer's directions. Alternatively, freeze in a rigid container until half-frozen, then beat well and transfer to 8 individual dariole molds. Freeze for 3–4 hours until solid or until required.

▧ Beat the egg whites with a pinch of salt until stiff, then beat in the sugar a spoonful at a time until thick and glossy.

▧ Unmold each ice cream on to a slice of jelly roll and place on a large cookie sheet. Cover each ice cream completely with about one-eighth of the meringue and place in the oven, preheated to the hottest setting, for about 2 minutes until just starting to be tinged brown.

▧ Serve at once with a pear leaf pressed into the top of each dessert.

VARIATIONS

INDIVIDUAL APPLE ALASKAS

Use 1 pound well-flavored eating apples instead of the pears. Peel, core and dice the apples, then cook over a gentle heat with half the sugar and the lemon juice until just tender. Leave to cool, then continue as above.

SIMPLE BAKED ALASKA

SERVES 4 – 6

≈

....

1 pint ice cream of your choice

5 ounce piece of cake, measuring approx. 7 × 3½ × ¾ inches

3 egg whites

pinch of salt

6 tbsp sugar

2 tbsp toasted slivered almonds

....

▧ Shape the ice cream into a rectangle about ½ inch smaller all around than the cake. Return the ice cream to the freezer.

▧ Beat the egg whites with a pinch of salt until stiff, then beat in the sugar a spoonful at a time until thick and glossy.

▧ Place the cake on a cookie sheet and position the ice cream on top. Spread the meringue on top to completely encase the ice cream and sprinkle with the almonds.

▧ Bake in a preheated oven set at the highest setting for 3–4 minutes until tinged golden brown.

▧ Serve at once.

Individual pear Alaskas

PLUM AND PRALINE ICE-CREAM CAKE

S E R V E S   1 2 – 1 4

≈

. . . .

CRUMB CRUST

heaped 1¾ cups graham cracker crumbs

6 tbsp unsalted butter, melted

PLUM LAYER

1 pound fresh plums, halved and pits removed

1 tbsp water

heaped 1 cup superfine sugar

1 tbsp liquid glucose

2 tbsp lemon juice

2 tbsp ruby port

5 egg yolks

1¼ cups heavy cream, lightly whipped

PRALINE AND CINNAMON LAYER

3 eggs, separated

6 tbsp sugar

1 cup praline (see right)

1 tsp ground cinnamon

3 tbsp brandy

1¼ cups heavy cream, whipped

whipped cream and fresh plum slices, to decorate

. . . .

▨ Line the sides of an 8-inch springform pan with a double thickness of waxed paper. Combine the cracker crumbs and butter and press onto the bottom of the pan. Chill.

▨ To make the plum layer, place the plums, water, ¼ cup sugar, liquid glucose and lemon juice in a saucepan and simmer over a gentle heat until the plums are soft – about 15 minutes. Leave to go cold, then puree in a blender and stir in the port.

▨ Beat the egg yolks and the remaining sugar in a bowl set over a saucepan of simmering water until pale and thick. Remove from the heat and continue beating until cool. Fold in the plum puree and cream.

▨ Freeze the mixture in an ice-cream machine according to the manufacturer's directions. Alternatively, freeze in a rigid container until partially frozen, then beat well. Transfer the mixture to the prepared pan, level the surface and freeze while the second layer is being made.

▨ To make the praline and cinnamon layer, beat the egg yolks and ¼ cup superfine sugar in a heatproof bowl set over a saucepan of simmering water until thick and pale. Remove from the heat and beat until cool. Fold in the praline, cinnamon, brandy and cream.

▨ Beat the egg whites until stiff, then beat in the remaining sugar a spoonful at a time. Fold into the praline mixture and pour on top of the plum layer. Freeze for 6–8 hours until firm or until required.

▨ Unmold and serve decorated with whirls of whipped cream and thin slices of fresh plum.

PRALINE

Place equal quantities of unblanched almonds and superfine sugar in a saucepan and cook over a medium heat until the sugar has dissolved. Increase the heat and cook the sugar until rich caramel in color. During this time, the almonds will have roasted to a light golden color. Transfer the mixture to a lightly greased cookie sheet and leave to go cold. Roughly break up the almond mixture, then crush to a fairly fine powder in a food processor or with a rolling pin. Store in an airtight container until required.

Plum and praline ice-cream cake

LEMON ICE-BOX CAKE

S E R V E S   8 – 1 0

≈

This is one of the simplest ice creams to make. It never becomes really hard in the freezer and cuts quite easily once unmolded.

. . . .

1¼ cups heavy cream
¾ cup confectioners' sugar, sifted
3 egg whites
finely grated peel and juice of 2
medium-sized lemons
8 ladyfingers

. . . .

▓ Whip the cream with ¼ cup of the sugar until just stiff. Beat the egg whites until stiff, then beat in the remaining sugar a spoonful at a time. Stir the lemon peel and juice into the cream, then fold in the egg whites.

▓ Line a 9-×5-×3-inch loaf pan with plastic wrap and make a layer with one-third of the lemon mixture. Arrange 4 ladyfingers on top, and continue layering until all the mixture and ladyfingers have been used up. Level the surface and freeze for 6–8 hours until solid or until required.

▓ Unmold and cut into thick slices to serve.

BISCUIT TORTONI

S E R V E S   8 – 1 0

≈

This distinctive dessert was originally made at the Tortoni Restaurant in Paris.

. . . .

2⅓ cups crumbled macaroons
6 tbsp medium-dry sherry
2 cups light cream
2 cups heavy cream
macaroons, to serve (optional)

. . . .

▓ Place I cup of the macaroons, the sherry and the light cream in a bowl and leave to one side for 15 minutes. Whip the heavy cream until it just holds its shape, then fold in the reserved cream mixture.

▓ Transfer to a 9-×5-×3-inch loaf pan lined on the bottom with waxed paper and freeze for 6–8 hours until solid or until required.

▓ Unmold on to a chopping board and leave to soften for a few minutes. Finely crush the remaining macaroons and press onto the surface of the ice cream until evenly coated. Freeze until required.

▓ Cut into thick slices and serve with extra macaroons, if desired.

TOP *Biscuit Tortoni;*
BOTTOM *Lemon ice-box cake*

IN THE COOLER

The recipes in this chapter require chilling in order to set or, in the case of cream-based desserts, to produce the desired final texture. Most are based on custard, cream, gelatin or fresh fruit.

An egg custard is made from the simplest ingredients — fresh eggs, sugar and milk — often with the addition of flavorings such as vanilla, coffee or citrus peels. The preparation of an egg custard is simple, but the actual cooking requires perfect timing and the correct amount of heat: if cooked too quickly at too high a temperature, a baked custard may develop a bubbly texture, while a custard sauce will almost certainly curdle.

A microwave oven is particularly useful for cooking egg-custard sauces. Use a plastic pitcher or bowl rather than a glass or china one, which can get very hot, and cook the custard on a medium-high setting, beating every 30 seconds until thick enough to coat the back of a wooden spoon. The time taken to make an egg custard is affected by the quantities of ingredients used, and guidelines are given in each of the recipes that follow.

Most of the quick recipes in this chapter incorporate whipped cream as a base and should always be served chilled. The fruit desserts also benefit from being well chilled: the gelatin-based desserts are left to set overnight, while the fruit in recipes such as Fresh figs with orange and honey marinate as they chill, so the flavor is enhanced.

CONTENTS

CRÈME CARAMEL

SERVES 8

≈

. . . .

Always make this dessert a day ahead so it has plenty of time to chill. This allows the caramel to become liquid again, giving the dessert its traditional sauce.

. . . .

CARAMEL

6 tbsp granulated sugar

3 tbsp water

CUSTARD

2½ cups milk or light cream

1 vanilla bean, split

4 eggs

3 tbsp superfine sugar

. . . .

▨ Dissolve the sugar in the water over a gentle heat, then bring to a boil and boil until deep caramel in color. Pour immediately into a 3¾-cup soufflé dish and turn the dish so that the bottom is evenly coated with the caramel. Set aside.

▨ Place the milk and vanilla bean in a saucepan and bring just to a boil. Remove from the heat and leave to infuse for at least 15 minutes. Remove the vanilla bean. Beat together the eggs and sugar and stir in the milk. Strain the custard into the soufflé dish.

▨ Place the soufflé dish in a roasting pan and pour in hot water to come at least halfway up the sides of the dish. Cook in a preheated 275°F oven for 1½–2 hours until the center is just firm to the touch. Remove from the oven and lift out of the roasting pan. Leave to cool, then chill overnight.

▨ Unmold on to a serving plate with a generous lip that will catch the caramel sauce.

APPLE SYLLABUBS

SERVES 6

≈

. . . .

finely grated peel and juice of 1 small orange

⅔ cup apple cider or applejack

3 tbsp superfine sugar

1¼ cups heavy cream

. . . .

▨ Combine the orange peel and juice, cider and sugar in a bowl. Add the cream and beat until the mixture becomes thick enough to hold the trail of the beaters Pour into individual glasses and chill for 1–2 hours.

SHERRY SYLLABUBS

SERVES 6

≈

. . . .

⅔ cup medium-dry sherry

¼ cup superfine sugar

2 tbsp lemon juice

2 tsp finely grated lemon peel

1¼ cups heavy cream

. . . .

▨ Place the sherry, sugar, lemon juice and peel in a bowl. Leave to infuse for at least 30 minutes.

▨ Add the cream and beat until the mixture stands in soft peaks. Transfer to individual glasses and chill for 1–2 hours before serving.

TOP *Apple syllabubs;*
BOTTOM *Crème caramel*

MANGO RIPPLE

SERVES 6 – 8

≈

Mangoes must always be ripe in order to impart the very best of their flavor to any dessert.

....

2 large, ripe mangoes, each weighing about
1 ¼ pounds

⅔ cup sugar syrup (*see page* 60)

juice of 3 limes

2 envelopes unflavored gelatin

2 tbsp water

⅔ cup heavy cream

2 egg whites

pinch of salt

¼ cup superfine sugar

....

▨ Peel the mangoes and cut away the flesh from each seed. Puree the mangoes in a blender. Mix one-third of the puree with the sugar syrup and the juice of 2 limes to make a sauce.

▨ Over a very gentle heat, dissolve the gelatin in the water and remaining lime juice, then stir in the remaining mango puree. Chill for about 1 hour until beginning to set.

▨ Whip the cream until it just holds its shape. Beat the egg whites with a pinch of salt until stiff, then beat in the sugar a little at a time. Fold the cream and egg-white mixture into the mango puree.

▨ Transfer the mixture to a serving dish. Drizzle a little of the mango sauce on the surface and swirl a skewer through the mixture to give a decorative effect. Chill for 3–4 hours until set.

▨ Serve the remaining sauce separately.

PEACH, HONEY AND YOGURT FOOLS

SERVES 4

≈

....

2 ¼ cups natural set yogurt

2 tbsp sunflower seeds

4 tbsp set honey

4 medium-sized ripe peaches, peeled,
pitted and chopped

....

▨ Combine all the ingredients together and divide between 4 individual glasses. Chill until required.

VARIATION

STRAWBERRY AND BANANA FOOL

Replace the peaches in the above recipe with heaped 1 ½ cups sliced strawberries and 1 large, ripe banana, peeled and mashed with ¼ cup superfine sugar. Omit the honey. Continue as above.

LEFT *Peach, honey and yogurt fools;*
RIGHT *Mango ripple*

PERUVIAN CREAMS

SERVES 6

≈

Milk infused with fresh coffee has a wonderful flavor: the strength of the flavor depends on the amount of time the milk is left to infuse with the coffee.

. . . .

2½ cups milk

I tbsp freshly ground coffee

¼ cup superfine sugar

4 eggs

6 tbsp apricot or peach jam, sieved

⅔ cup heavy cream, lightly whipped

6 ounces semisweet chocolate, grated

. . . .

▨ Heat the milk, coffee and sugar in a saucepan until just below boiling point. Remove from the heat and leave to infuse for at least 15 minutes, then pour through a fine strainer. Beat the eggs and pour the coffee-flavored milk on top. Stir well, then strain into 6 individual ramekin dishes.

▨ Place the dishes in a roasting pan and pour hot water around them to come at least halfway up their sides. Cook in a preheated 275°F oven for about 40 minutes, until just set.

▨ Remove from the pan and leave to cool.

▨ Chill the creams until required, then spread each one with a little apricot jam. Top with whipped cream and grated chocolate.

DAMSON MOUSSE

SERVES 6 – 8

≈

Imported damsons give this mousse a particularly pretty pink color, but any other plums may be used. The prepared mousse can be frozen, either in a large quantity or in individual portions. Allow the mousse to freeze, uncovered, until the surface is solid, then wrap and store. When required, remove the wrapping and thaw in the refrigerator for several hours. Before serving, check the mousse with a fine skewer to make sure that it has thawed completely.

. . . .

I pound damsons or other plums

¼ cup granulated sugar

2 eggs, separated

2 tsp unflavored gelatin

2 tbsp water

⅔ cup heavy cream, whipped

2 tbsp superfine sugar

. . . .

▨ Cook the damsons with the sugar over a gentle heat until tender – about 15 minutes. Leave to cool, then remove the pits and puree the flesh in a blender. Beat in the egg yolks.

▨ Dissolve the gelatin in the water over a very gentle heat and stir into the damson puree. Leave until cold, then fold in the whipped cream.

▨ Beat the egg whites until stiff, then beat in the superfine sugar a little at a time. Fold into the damson mixture and transfer to a serving dish, or to individual dishes. Chill for 3–4 hours until set.

TOP *Damson mousse;*

BOTTOM *Peruvian creams*

VANILLA AND COFFEE BAVAROIS

SERVES 6

≈

....

3 egg yolks

¼ cup superfine sugar

1¼ cups milk

1½ tbsp unflavored gelatin

3 tbsp water

1 tsp vanilla essence

2 tsp instant coffee, dissolved in a few drops
of boiling water

⅔ cup heavy cream, lightly whipped

2 egg whites

....

▓ Beat the egg yolks with half the sugar until thick and pale. Heat the milk to just below boiling point and pour onto the egg-yolk mixture. Cook in a heatproof bowl set over a saucepan of simmering water until the custard has thickened enough to coat the back of a wooden spoon. Alternatively, cook in a microwave oven on a medium-high setting for 2–3 minutes, stirring every 30 seconds. Dissolve the gelatin in the water over a gentle heat, then stir into the custard.

▓ Divide the custard into 2 equal portions. Add the vanilla to one portion and the coffee to the other. Chill both mixtures for about 30 minutes, until just on the point of setting, then fold half the whipped cream into each portion.

▓ Stiffly beat the egg whites, then beat in the reserved sugar a little at a time. Fold half of this mixture into each custard.

▓ Spoon both mixtures into a lightly greased 3¾-cup mold, alternating the colors to give a marbled effect. Cover and chill for several hours, or preferably overnight, until set.

▓ Unmold on to a serving plate.

KIWI-FRUIT BAVAROIS

SERVES 6–8

≈

A *few drops of green food coloring may be added to the kiwi fruit puree to enhance the color, if desired.*

....

4 ripe kiwi fruit, peeled and chopped

6 tbsp superfine sugar

3 egg yolks

1¼ cups milk

1 tbsp unflavored gelatin

3 tbsp water

1¼ cups heavy cream, lightly whipped

kiwi fruit wedges, to decorate

....

▓ Puree the kiwi fruit in a blender with 2 tbsp of the sugar, then pass through a fine strainer to remove most of the seeds. Place the puree in a saucepan and cook gently for 5 minutes, stirring occasionally. Leave to cool.

▓ Beat the egg yolks with the remaining sugar until thick and pale. Heat the milk to just below boiling point and pour onto the egg-yolk mixture. Cook in a heatproof bowl set over a saucepan of simmering water until the custard has thickened enough to coat the back of a wooden spoon. Alternatively, cook in a microwave oven on a medium-high setting for 2–3 minutes, stirring every 30 seconds until thickened.

▓ Dissolve the gelatin in the water over a very gentle heat and stir into the custard. Stir in the kiwi fruit puree.

▓ Chill the mixture until just on the point of setting, then fold in the cream and transfer to a lightly greased 3¾-cup mold. Chill for about 6 hours, or preferably overnight, until set.

▓ Unmold the bavarois on to a serving plate and decorate with the kiwi fruit wedges.

Vanilla and coffee bavarois

FLORENTINE ZUCCOTTO

SERVES 10

≈

....

CHOCOLATE CAKE

1½ tsp vinegar or lemon juice
½ cup milk
1 cup all-purpose flour
½ tsp baking soda
2 tbsp cocoa powder
¼ cup unsalted butter
½ cup plus 2 tbsp sugar
1 egg

FILLING

4 tbsp sugar syrup (*see page* 60)
2 tbsp kirsch
2 cups heavy cream
¼ cup confectioners' sugar, sifted
heaped 1 cup blackberries
heaped 1 cup black currants
confectioners' sugar, to decorate

....

▤ Combine the vinegar and milk. Sift the dry ingredients together. Cream the butter with half the sugar until pale. Beat in the egg, followed by the remaining sugar. Stir in the milk and flour mixtures alternately.

▤ Transfer the mixture to a greased deep 8-inch cake pan lined on the bottom with baking parchment. Bake in a preheated 350°F oven for about 40 minutes until risen and firm to the touch. Cool on a wire rack. When completely cold, cut into 3 layers.

▤ Cut and trim the chocolate cake as necessary and use it to line the bottom and sides of a 6¼-cup charlotte mold, leaving sufficient cake to make a bottom. Combine the sugar syrup and kirsch and sprinkle some over the cake to moisten it.

▤ Whip the cream with the sugar until stiff, then fold in the fruit. Spoon the mixture into the lined pan. Top with the remaining cake and moisten with the remaining syrup. Press down firmly, cover and chill overnight.

▤ Unmold on to a plate and dust with sugar.

COEURS À LA CRÈME

SERVES 4

≈

These delicate soft-cheese desserts are delicious served with any summer berries. Traditional heart-shaped molds are available to shape them in, but they may be made in other small containers.

....

1 cup cottage cheese, sieved
4 tbsp heavy cream, whipped
2 egg whites
3 tbsp superfine sugar
extra superfine sugar, for sprinkling
light cream
4 small pansies, to decorate (optional)

....

▤ Combine the cottage cheese and whipped cream. Stiffly beat the egg whites, then beat in the sugar a little at a time. Fold the egg-white mixture into the cheese mixture until evenly combined.

▤ Divide the mixture between 4 coeur à la crème molds lined with cheesecloth, then level the surfaces. Fold any overhanging cheesecloth on top, then place the molds on a tray and chill overnight. If using other small molds, line them with cheesecloth and place them upside down on the tray so they can drain. Alternatively, pierce some holes in the bottoms of the molds so the liquid can drain away.

▤ Unmold the desserts on to individual plates, sprinkle with superfine sugar and pour light cream around each one. Decorate each dessert with a small pansy.

Coeurs à la crème

CREAMED RICE MOUSSES

SERVES 6

≈

· ·

<u>RICE CREAM</u>
¼ cup pudding rice
2½ cups milk
pared peel of 1 lemon
¼ cup superfine sugar
1¼ cups light cream
2 envelopes unflavored gelatin
3 tbsp water
2 egg whites
<u>LEMON SAUCE</u>
¼ cup superfine sugar
1 tbsp cornstarch
1¼ cups water
2 tbsp unsalted butter
1 tsp finely grated lemon peel
3 tbsp lemon juice
small pieces of angelica, to decorate

· ·

▓ Cook the rice in boiling water for 5 minutes. Drain and place in a saucepan with the milk, lemon peel and half the sugar. Bring to a boil, then reduce the heat and simmer, covered, for about 30 minutes until tender. Remove the lemon peel and stir in the light cream.

▓ Dissolve the gelatin in the water over a gentle heat and stir into the rice mixture. Chill for about 30 minutes until just on the point of setting. Beat the egg whites until stiff, then gradually beat in the remaining sugar.

▓ Fold in the rice mixture and divide it between 6 individual molds. Level the surfaces and chill for 2–3 hours until set.

▓ To make the sauce, mix together the sugar, cornstarch and water in a small saucepan and bring to a boil, stirring constantly. Simmer for 1–2 minutes, then remove from the heat and stir in the remaining ingredients. Leave to cool.

▓ Unmold the desserts and decorate with small pieces of angelica. Serve with the lemon sauce.

SPICED CRANBERRY AND APPLE CREAMS

SERVES 6

≈

· ·

1 cup cranberries
2 tbsp granulated sugar
1¼ cups apple juice
3 tbsp honey
½ tsp ground cinnamon
¼ tsp ground allspice
2 tbsp semolina
1 tbsp lemon juice
2 tbsp heavy cream, whipped
1 eating apple, cored and finely chopped
fresh apple slices, to decorate

· ·

▓ Place the cranberries, sugar, apple juice, honey, spices, semolina and lemon juice in a saucepan. Bring to a boil, stirring all the time until the mixture thickens, then simmer for a further 2–3 minutes, stirring constantly. Transfer the mixture to a bowl and leave to go cold.

▓ Fold in the whipped cream and chopped apple and transfer to individual glasses. Chill for 2–3 hours or until required.

▓ Decorate with fresh apple slices just before serving.

TOP *Spiced cranberry and apple creams;*
BOTTOM *Creamed rice mousses*

CHILLED ZABAGLIONE

SERVES 4

≈

....

4 egg yolks
4 tbsp superfine sugar
½ cup Marsala
1 tsp unflavored gelatin
2 tbsp water
½ cup heavy cream, lightly whipped
8 macaroons
12 orange segments
toasted slivered almonds, to decorate

....

▨ Place the egg yolks, sugar and Marsala in a large heatproof bowl and whisk over a saucepan of simmering water until thick and foamy. Remove from the heat and continue whisking until cool.

▨ Dissolve the gelatin with the water in a bowl set over a saucepan of simmering water. Cool slightly, then add the cream and whisk until the mixture holds the trail of the whisk. Fold the whipped cream into the Marsala mixture.

▨ Place 2 macaroons and 3 orange segments in each of 4 sundae glasses and top with the Marsala mixture. Chill for about 1 hour before serving.

▨ Just before serving, decorate the desserts with a few toasted slivered almonds.

ST. CLEMENT'S BOODLE

SERVES 6

≈

Boodle's was one of the oldest gentlemen's clubs in London and Orange boodle was a popular favorite there in the Twenties. You can either present the dessert in one large bowl or in individual serving dishes as below. Make sure you allow plenty of time for it to chill so the orange and lemon juices are well absorbed into the ladyfingers.

....

finely grated peel and juice of 2 large oranges
finely grated peel and juice of 1 large lemon
¼ cup superfine sugar
1¼ cups heavy cream
6 ladyfingers, sliced

....

▨ Combine the fruit peels and juices with the sugar. Beat the cream until stiff, then slowly beat in the fruit-juice mixture.

▨ Divide the ladyfingers between 6 individual glass dishes and pour the cream mixture on top. Chill for 4–6 hours until set.

LEFT *Chilled zabaglione;*
RIGHT *St. Clement's boodle*

CARAMEL CHARLOTTE RUSSE

SERVES 6 - 8

≈

Ladyfingers delicately flavored with brandy encase a rich caramel filling in this variation of a classic dessert. Thinly sliced jelly roll may be used as an alternative jacket, in which case a bowl should be used as a mold.

. . . .

½ cup superfine sugar

4 egg yolks

1¼ cups plus 3 tbsp milk

2 tsp unflavored gelatin

2 tbsp brandy

12–14 ladyfingers

1¼ cups heavy cream

1 tsp lemon juice

TO DECORATE

whipped cream

caramel scribbles (*see right*)

. . . .

▨ Place 6 tbsp of the sugar in a small saucepan with 2 tbsp water and dissolve over a gentle heat. Increase the heat and cook until the syrup becomes golden caramel in color. Remove from the heat and carefully add 2 tbsp hot water, swirling it in the pan to dissolve the caramel.

▨ Beat the egg yolks with the remaining sugar until pale, then beat in the caramel syrup. Add 1¼ cups milk to the saucepan in which the caramel was made and heat gently to just below boiling point. This will dissolve any caramel left in the saucepan. Stir the milk into the egg mixture, then cook in the top of a double boiler until the custard has thickened enough to coat the back of a wooden spoon – about 20 minutes. Alternatively, cook in a microwave oven on a medium-high setting for about 5 minutes, stirring every 30 seconds.

▨ Dissolve the gelatin in 3 tbsp water over a very gentle heat. Add to the custard. Chill the custard for 30–45 minutes until just beginning to set.

▨ Mix the remaining milk and 1 tbsp of the brandy and quickly dip the ladyfingers in to soften them slightly. Use the ladyfingers to line the sides of a lightly greased 6¼-cup charlotte mold, pressing them carefully against the sides.

▨ Whip the cream with the remaining brandy and the lemon juice until it has a soft dropping consistency. Fold into the caramel-custard mixture and transfer to the lined mold. Chill for at least 4–6 hours, or preferably overnight, until set.

▨ Unmold on to a serving plate and pipe with extra whipped cream, then decorate with caramel scribbles.

VARIATION

CARAMEL SCRIBBLES

Lightly grease a cookie sheet. Dissolve ½ cup granulated or superfine sugar with 4 tbsp water in a saucepan over a very gentle heat. Increase the heat and cook until rich caramel in color. Using a greased teaspoon, drizzle random patterns onto the cookie sheet and leave to harden; at this stage, the caramel scribbles will lift easily from the cookie sheet.

These decorations may be made 2–3 hours in advance and kept between sheets of waxed paper in an airtight container until ready for use.

Caramel charlotte Russe

ORANGE MOUSSES WITH FRESH LYCHEES

S E R V E S   6

≈

. . . .

MOUSSE

¼ cup superfine sugar

6 tbsp water

finely grated peel and juice of 1 orange

1 tbsp lemon juice

2 eggs, separated

1½ tsp unflavored gelatin

⅔ cup heavy cream

LYCHEE AND ORANGE SAUCE

coarsely grated peel of ½ large orange

juice of 1 large orange

1 tsp lemon juice

2 tbsp superfine sugar

16 fresh lychees, peeled, pitted and
coarsely chopped

. . . .

◼ To make the mousse, dissolve the sugar in 4 tbsp of the water over a gentle heat. Add the orange peel and juice and the lemon juice and boil for 3 minutes.

◼ Place the egg yolks in a food processor and process for 30 seconds. Add the fruit syrup and continue working the processor for 1 minute. Dissolve the gelatin in the remaining water and pour this onto the egg mixture while processing. Transfer to a bowl and chill for about 30 minutes, until just on the point of setting.

◼ Lightly whip the cream, and beat the egg whites until stiff. Beat the orange mixture until it is smooth, then fold in the cream and egg whites. Transfer to 6 individual ⅔-cup molds and chill until set.

◼ Place the orange peel in a saucepan and just cover with cold water. Bring to a boil, then drain immediately. Return the orange peel to the saucepan with the orange and lemon juices and the sugar. Simmer for about 5 minutes until slightly syrupy. Remove from the heat and stir in the lychees. Leave to cool.

◼ Unmold the mousses and surround with the sauce.

CHOCOLATE AND RICOTTA MOUSSES

S E R V E S   4

≈

. . . .

1 cup ricotta cheese

5 tbsp maple syrup

2 ounces semisweet chocolate, melted

1 egg white

⅔ cup heavy cream

ground cinnamon or cocoa powder, to
sprinkle

. . . .

◼ Beat the ricotta cheese with 4 tbsp of the maple syrup until smooth. Stir in the chocolate until evenly combined. Transfer to 4 small glasses.

◼ Beat the egg white until stiff. Whip the cream with the remaining maple syrup until stiff, then fold in the egg white to make a chantilly cream.

◼ Spoon the cream on top of the chocolate mixture and chill for 1–2 hours. Sprinkle with ground cinnamon or cocoa powder just before serving.

TOP *Chocolate and ricotta mousses;*
BOTTOM *Orange mousses with fresh lychees*

TRIO OF MELON WITH GINGER SYRUP

SERVES 4

≈

....

1 pound wedge of watermelon
1 pound charentais melon
1 pound honeydew melon
⅔ cup sugar syrup (*see below*)
2 tbsp finely chopped preserved ginger
1 tbsp lemon juice

....

▪ Using a melon-ball cutter, scoop out balls from the 3 wedges of melon and put them in a bowl.
▪ Place the sugar syrup, ginger and lemon juice in a small saucepan and simmer for 5 minutes. Cool and pour over the melon balls. Chill for several hours or until required. Stir well and transfer to a serving dish.

SUGAR SYRUP

MAKES ABOUT 3 CUPS

≈

....

heaped 1 cup granulated sugar
2½ cups water
2 tbsp lemon juice

....

▪ Dissolve the sugar in the water over a gentle heat. Add the lemon juice and bring to a boil. Cool the syrup and then strain it.

FRESH FIGS WITH ORANGE AND HONEY

SERVES 4

≈

For the best results, always choose ripe figs for this recipe.

....

12 fresh figs, washed
coarsely grated peel and juice of 1 orange
4 tbsp honey
½ tsp ground cinnamon
fresh cream, to serve

....

▪ Cut a deep cross in each fig and place in a baking dish. Sprinkle with the orange peel and juice, honey and cinnamon and bake in a preheated 350°F oven for 10 minutes. Leave to cool, then chill for 3–4 hours or until required.
▪ Serve with cream for pouring over.
(*See picture, pages 40–41.*)

Trio of melon with ginger syrup

CLASSIC LEMON SOUFFLÉ

SERVES 6

≈

A cold soufflé is really a type of mousse that has been made to set above the level of the serving dish, so it resembles its name-sake, the hot soufflé, in appearance. It can be made the day before it is required and left to set in the refrigerator.

. . . .

4 eggs, separated
½ cup superfine sugar
4 tsp finely grated lemon peel
8 tbsp fresh lemon juice
1 tbsp unflavored gelatin
3 tbsp water
¾ cup heavy cream, lightly whipped

TO DECORATE
whipped cream
mimosa balls
julienne strips of lemon peel

. . . .

▪ Wrap a double thickness of waxed paper around a 5½-inch diameter (3¾-cup capacity) soufflé dish so that it extends about 2 inches above the top of the dish. Ensure that the waxed paper collar is tight and firmly secured around the soufflé dish. Place on a plate or tray.

▪ Place the egg yolks, sugar, lemon peel and juice in a large bowl and beat over a saucepan of simmering water for 10–15 minutes until thick and foamy. Remove from the heat and continue beating until cool.

▪ Dissolve the gelatin in the water over a very gentle heat and fold into the lemon mixture.

▪ Chill the mixture until cold, but before it begins to set – about 30 minutes – then fold in the cream. Beat the egg whites until stiff and fold them into the mixture. Transfer to the prepared soufflé dish and chill for 4–6 hours, or preferably overnight, until set.

▪ Carefully peel off the lining paper. Decorate the top of the soufflé with whipped-cream rosettes, mimosa balls and julienne strips of lemon peel. If desired, finely chopped nuts may be pressed into the "risen" edges of the soufflé.

VARIATIONS

ORANGE SOUFFLÉ

Omit the lemon peel and juice in the recipe and instead use the finely grated peel of 2 oranges and 4 tbsp orange juice, plus 2 tbsp lemon juice or orange liqueur. Follow the method described in the recipe. Decorate with julienne strips of orange peel and pieces of fresh orange or walnuts.

COFFEE SOUFFLÉ

Omit the lemon peel and juice in the recipe and instead use 6 tbsp strong, fresh black coffee. Follow the method described in the recipe. Decorate with chocolate leaves (see page 10) or sugared coffee beans.

Classic lemon soufflé

JELLIED FRUIT TERRINE

SERVES 10

≈

The proportion of gelatin to fruit juice in this recipe is relatively high as the gelatin has to support several layers of fruit. If you want to serve this terrine straight out of a serving dish without unmolding, reduce the amount of gelatin to 4 tsp.

2 tbsp unflavored gelatin

3 cups white grape juice

heaped 1 cup each of raspberries and strawberries

1½ cups pitted cherries

½ cup red currants

light cream, to serve (optional)

■ Dissolve the gelatin in ⅔ cup of the grape juice over a very gentle heat, then stir in the remaining grape juice. Pour some of the juice into a 9-×5-×3-inch loaf pan to make a thin layer about ¼ inch deep. Chill for about 30 minutes until set.

■ Arrange a layer of raspberries on the gelatin. Carefully spoon enough juice over the raspberries to just cover them. Chill for about 1 hour until set.

■ Continue layering the fruit and juice, allowing each layer to set before commencing on the next one and finishing with the red currants. Chill for several hours, preferably overnight, until completely set.

■ Unmold the terrine and serve in slices with light cream for pouring over if desired.

VARIATIONS

The raspberries and strawberries in the above recipe may be replaced with any other soft fruit such as blueberries, blackberries, black currants or wild strawberries.

APPLE CHARTREUSE

SERVES 8

≈

2 pounds eating apples

1¼ cups water

1 tsp lemon juice

1½ cups granulated sugar

⅔ cup assorted chopped candied fruit,

light cream, to serve (optional)

■ Pare and core the apples. Place all the trimmings in a saucepan with the water and simmer for 10 minutes. Slice the apples thickly and toss with the lemon juice. Keep covered until required.

■ Strain the cooking water and discard the trimmings. Place the apple water in a large, shallow pan. Add the sugar and dissolve over a gentle heat. Bring to a boil and boil for 5 minutes. Add the apple slices and cook fairly rapidly, stirring from time to time, for about 20 minutes or until all the liquid has evaporated.

■ Stir well, add the candied fruit and pour into a dampened 8½-×4½-×2½-inch loaf pan or mold. Chill for several hours, or preferably overnight, until set.

■ Unmold and cut into slices. Serve with light cream for pouring over, if desired.

TOP *Jellied fruit terrine,*

BOTTOM *Apple chartreuse*

CHILLED STUFFED APPLES

SERVES 6

≈

Once cooked, these apples may be left to marinate in the syrup for several days. Turn them from time to time so they become evenly colored.

. . . .

1¼ cups dry red wine

pared peel of ½ lemon

juice of 1 lemon

½ cup granulated sugar

1 cinnamon stick

6 large eating apples, pared and cored

2 tbsp finely chopped raisins

1 tbsp roasted and finely chopped filberts

1 tbsp roasted and finely chopped blanched almonds

½ cup heavy cream, lightly whipped

6 apple-mint leaves, to decorate

. . . .

■ Place the wine, lemon peel and juice, sugar and cinnamon in a saucepan and bring to a boil. Add the apples, reduce the heat and simmer, covered, for about 10 minutes until just tender.

■ Remove the apples from the pan and stand them in a dish. Strain the juice over the apples and add the raisins. Leave to go cold, then chill until required, turning the apples from time to time to give them an even color.

■ Place each apple in an individual dish. Strain the juice and reserve the raisins. Add the raisins and the roasted nuts to the cream. Using a pastry bag fitted with a large, plain tip, fill the apples with the cream mixture, piling any remaining mixture on top.

■ Decorate each apple with a mint leaf. Spoon a little juice around each apple and chill until required.

CHESTNUT AND BRANDY CREAMS

SERVES 6

≈

Fresh chestnuts are ideal for this recipe but canned whole chestnuts may also be used. If dried chestnuts are used, they should be soaked overnight before cooking. The marron glacés suggested for decoration are candied chestnuts, a speciality of France. You will find them in gourmet food stores.

. . . .

10 ounces peeled and cooked chestnuts

⅔ cup milk

6 tbsp superfine sugar

2 tbsp brandy

⅔ cup heavy cream, lightly whipped

2 egg whites

slices of marron glacé, to decorate (optional)

. . . .

■ Puree the chestnuts, milk, half the sugar and the brandy in a blender until smooth. Fold in the whipped cream.

■ Beat the egg whites until stiff, then beat in the remaining sugar a spoonful at a time until thick and glossy. Fold into the chestnut mixture. Transfer to individual glasses and chill for 1–2 hours or until required.

■ Decorate each serving with slices of marron glacé if you like.

TOP *Chestnut and brandy creams;*
BOTTOM *Chilled stuffed apples*

RASPBERRY SYLLABUB TRIFLES

SERVES 6

≈

. . . .

1 ½ cups raspberries

2 tbsp confectioners' sugar

⅔ cup rosé wine

2 tsp finely grated lemon peel

2 tbsp lemon juice

¼ cup superfine sugar

2 tbsp Framboise (raspberry liqueur)

1 ¼ cups heavy cream

3 ladyfingers

2 tbsp raspberry jam

. . . .

▪ Puree half the raspberries with the confectioners' sugar. Pass through a fine strainer to remove the seeds.
▪ Place the rosé wine, lemon peel and juice, superfine sugar and Framboise in a large bowl.
▪ Add the cream and beat until the mixture is thick enough to show the trail of the beaters. Fold in the raspberry puree until evenly combined.
▪ Split the ladyfingers and sandwich together with the jam. Cut each sponge sandwich into 4 pieces.
▪ Divide the ladyfinger pieces and the remaining raspberries between 6 individual glasses and pour the raspberry syllabub on top. Chill the desserts for 3–4 hours or until required.

GREENGAGE SYLLABUB TRIFLES

SERVES 8

≈

. . . .

1 pound greengages, pits removed

¼ cup granulated sugar

CUSTARD

1 ¼ cups light cream

2 strips pared lemon peel

3 egg yolks

2 tbsp superfine sugar

1 tsp cornstarch

SYLLABUB

1 ¼ cups heavy cream

¼ cup superfine sugar

1 tsp finely grated orange peel

2 tbsp orange juice

⅔ cup beer

. . . .

▪ Cook the greengages with the sugar over a gentle heat for 10–15 minutes until soft. Cool and puree in a blender. Spoon a little of the puree into 8 individual glasses.
▪ To make the custard, place the cream and lemon peel in a saucepan and bring just to a boil. Leave to one side. Beat together the egg yolks, sugar and cornstarch until pale and smooth, then stir in the cream and cook over the gentlest heat, stirring constantly, until the custard has thickened enough to coat the back of a wooden spoon. Alternatively, cook in a microwave oven on a medium-high setting for 2 minutes, stirring every 30 seconds until thickened. Strain the custard and pour a little of it into each glass. Chill.
▪ To make the syllabub, place all the ingredients for this in a bowl and beat until thickened. Divide the syllabub between the glasses and chill until required.

Raspberry syllabub trifles

JAPONAISE

SERVES 10-12

≈

....

1¾ cups finely ground blanched almonds
5 egg whites
2 tsp lemon juice
½ tsp almond essence
1 cup superfine sugar
¼ cup cornstarch
1 quantity coffee crème au beurre (*see right*)
1 quantity chocolate ganache (*see right*)

....

◻ Grease three 8-inch cake pans and line them on the bottom with foil.
◻ Place the ground almonds in a skillet and cook, stirring frequently, until golden. Leave to cool.
◻ Beat the egg whites until stiff, then beat in the lemon juice and almond essence. Beat in the sugar a spoonful at a time. Stir the cornstarch into the last spoonful of sugar and fold in with 1¼ cups of the ground almonds.
◻ Divide the mixture between the prepared pans and level the surfaces. Bake in a preheated 325°F oven for 30 minutes. Leave to go cold, then remove the lining papers.
◻ Sandwich 2 layers together with half of the coffee crème au beurre, then spread the top with all but 2 tbsp of the chocolate ganache and gently press the last layer on top. Cover the top and sides with the remaining coffee crème au beurre. Carefully press the remaining ground almonds on to the top and sides of the cake to completely cover it.
◻ Use the reserved chocolate ganache to pipe a design on top of the Japonaise. Chill until required.

COFFEE CRÈME AU BEURRE

≈

If chilled before use, this mixture loses its wonderful consistency. Once spread on a cake, however, it keeps perfectly in the refrigerator.

....

3 egg yolks
6 tbsp superfine sugar
5 tbsp milk
¾ cup unsalted butter, diced
2 tbsp strong black coffee

....

◻ Beat together the egg yolks and sugar until thick and pale. Heat the milk just to boiling point and pour onto the egg mixture. Cook over a saucepan of simmering water until the mixture thickens enough to coat the back of a wooden spoon. Strain and continue beating until cool. Beat in the butter a little at a time until thick, then beat in the coffee.

CHOCOLATE GANACHE

≈

....

½ cup heavy cream
4 ounces semisweet chocolate, broken into pieces

....

◻ Place the cream and chocolate in a saucepan and warm gently until the chocolate has melted. Beat well and transfer to a bowl. Leave to cool until firm. Whisk until smooth, then use as required.

Japonaise

CHOCOLATE TERRINE

SERVES 10-12

≈

....

NUT LAYER

⅓ cup blanched almonds

⅓ cup skinned filberts

3 egg whites

6 tbsp superfine sugar

I tbsp all-purpose flour, sifted

WHITE LAYER

5 ounces white chocolate

3 tbsp milk

1½ tsp unflavored gelatin

2 tbsp water

⅔ cup crème fraîche or soured cream

I egg white, stiffly beaten

DARK LAYER

6 ounces semisweet chocolate

2 tbsp strong fresh coffee

¼ cup unsalted butter

⅔ cup crème fraîche or soured cream

RASPBERRY COULIS

I pound raspberries

4 tbsp confectioners' sugar

fresh raspberries and raspberry leaves, to decorate (optional)

....

■ To make the crust, roast the nuts in a preheated 400°F oven for about 10 minutes, then grate or finely grind them. Beat the egg whites until stiff, then beat in the sugar a spoonful at a time. Fold in the remaining ingredients.

■ Spread the mixture in a 13-× 9-inch pan with the bottom and sides lined with waxed paper. Bake in a preheated 400°F oven for 20 minutes. Leave to cool in the pan.

■ Cut the nut cake into 3-inch strips and place one strip on the base of a lined 10- × 3-inch terrine dish.

■ Melt the white chocolate and milk over simmering water. Dissolve the gelatin in the water over a gentle heat and stir into the chocolate. Leave to cool and stir in the crème fraîche. Fold in the beaten egg white and transfer to the terrine. Level the surface and chill until just setting. Cover with a strip of nut cake.

■ Melt the semisweet chocolate with the coffee over simmering water. Remove from the heat and stir in the butter and crème fraîche. Transfer to the terrine and cover with a layer of nut cake. Chill until firm.

■ Puree together the raspberries and confectioners' sugar, then pass through a fine strainer to remove the seeds.

■ Unmold, decorate and serve with the coulis.

CHOCOLATE REFRIGERATOR CAKE

SERVES 8

≈

....

½ cup unsalted butter

½ cup soft brown sugar

4 ounces semisweet chocolate

I egg, beaten

2 cups coarsely crumbled graham crackers

4 tbsp chopped preserved ginger

⅓ cup toasted and chopped blanched almonds

TO DECORATE

whipped cream

pieces of stem ginger

....

■ Place the butter and sugar in a saucepan and heat gently until the sugar dissolves. Add the chocolate and stir until melted, then beat in the egg. Stir in the remaining ingredients and transfer to a 7- or 8-inch cake pan. Chill until set.

■ Unmold, cut into wedges and decorate.

TOP *Chocolate refrigerator cake;*
BOTTOM *Chocolate terrine*

COLD COMFORT

There is a fine dividing line between chilled food and cold food, and it is to some extent a matter of personal preference as to how a particular recipe should be served. Deep chilling tends to mask the flavor of many foods so that their full potential is not realized, and this is especially true of many recipes containing fruit. For this reason, it is suggested that the dishes in this chapter are served cold rather than chilled.

It is always useful to have a selection of recipes suitable for parties and other celebrations, and this chapter contains many spectacular and involved desserts appropriate for such occasions. Inevitably, their preparation tends to be rather time-consuming, but the results are well worth the effort.

In this section, those gateaux that are decorated with fresh cream should be kept in the refrigerator once they have been made. The same applies to the pies, which need to be stored in the refrigerator and served cold on the day of preparation.

Many of these recipes can be assembled in stages, as they include meringue, cake or cookie bases that can all be stored in airtight containers for several days after they have been made.

CONTENTS

RICH CHOCOLATE POTS

SERVES 8

≈

Use the best semisweet chocolate you can find for this recipe.

. . . .

6 egg yolks
2 tbsp superfine sugar
2 cups light cream
8 ounces semisweet chocolate, grated
4 tbsp liqueur of your choice (optional)

. . . .

▪ Beat together the egg yolks and sugar in a heatproof bowl. Warm the cream to just below boiling point and stir into the egg yolks.

▪ Transfer to a mixing bowl set over a saucepan of simmering water and cook until the mixture has thickened enough to coat the back of a wooden spoon. Alternatively, cook the custard in a microwave oven on a medium-high setting for about 3 minutes, stirring every 30 seconds, until the custard thickens.

▪ Add the grated chocolate and stir until melted and thoroughly incorporated. Stir in the liqueur, if using.

▪ Pass the mixture through a fine strainer and pour into 8 small cups. Chill for 4–6 hours or until required.

VARIATION

FUDGE AND BRANDY POTS

Replace the semisweet chocolate in the above recipe with 8 ounces milk chocolate-covered fudge bars. Melt these in the light cream over a gentle heat and continue as above. Use brandy or rum as a flavoring. Decorate with piped chocolate decorations (see right), if desired.

CHOCOLATE DESIGNS

Melt chocolate and fill a small pastry bag fitted with a plain writing tip. Draw a template of the chosen design and place it under a sheet of waxed paper set on a cookie sheet. Pipe the chocolate design following the line of the template. Continue until enough designs have been made. Leave the designs in a cool place until set, then carefully remove from the paper and use as required. The chocolate designs may be stored in an airtight container. Once you are more confident, you may like to pipe the chocolate designs freehand.

LEFT *Rich chocolate pots;*
RIGHT *Fudge and brandy pots*

FLOATING ISLANDS

SERVES 4 - 6

≈

Floating islands (Îles flottantes) must be one of the best-known French desserts. Its basic constituents are an egg-custard sauce and delicately poached meringues.

. . . .

CUSTARD SAUCE

4 egg yolks

I tsp cornstarch

¼ cup superfine sugar

2½ cups light cream or milk

6 passion fruit

2 tbsp Armagnac

MERINGUE ISLANDS

I egg white

pinch of salt

2 tbsp superfine sugar

2½ cups milk, for poaching

CARAMEL

¼ cup granulated sugar

2 tbsp water

. . . .

◼ Beat together the egg yolks, cornstarch and sugar in a heatproof bowl. Bring the cream just to boiling point, then stir into the egg-yolk mixture.

◼ Place the bowl over a saucepan of simmering water and cook, stirring frequently, until the mixture thickens. Pass through a fine strainer, cover and leave to cool.

◼ Cut the passion fruit in half and extract all the pulp and seeds. Pass through a fine strainer and collect the juice. Stir into the custard with the Armagnac and chill for 1–2 hours or until required.

◼ Beat the egg white with a pinch of salt until stiff. Beat in the sugar a little at a time until the mixture is thick and glossy.

◼ Heat the milk in a wide, shallow saucepan and drop teaspoonfuls of the mixture into the simmering milk. Poach for 2–3 minutes until just firm to the touch. Remove from the pan and drain on a dish towel. Con-

tinue poaching the "islands" until all the mixture has been used up.

◼ Spoon the custard sauce into individual dishes and arrange a few "islands" on top.

◼ Place the sugar and water in a saucepan and dissolve over a gentle heat. Increase the heat and cook without stirring until medium caramel in color. Immediately drizzle a little of the caramel over each dessert and serve at once.

VARIATION

A few thin slices of strawberry or segments of orange can be added to the custard sauce in place of the passion fruit and Armagnac. Try drizzling a thick fruit puree over the dessert instead of the caramel.

DRIED FRUIT COMPOTE

SERVES 6 - 8

≈

. . . .

I tbsp mango tea

2 cups assorted dried fruit

2 tbsp brown sugar

I tbsp lemon juice

2 bananas, peeled and sliced

. . . .

◼ Make the tea with 5 cups boiling water and leave to infuse for 5 minutes. Strain and place in a large saucepan.

◼ Rinse the fruit thoroughly and add to the saucepan with the sugar and lemon juice. Bring to a boil, then cover and simmer for 20 minutes, until the fruit is tender.

◼ Transfer to a serving dish and leave to go cold. Refrigerate until required. Just before serving, stir in the bananas.

Floating islands

POACHED PEARS IN SPICED CIDER

SERVES 4

≈

1¼ cups apple cider
pared peel of ½ lemon
juice of 1 lemon
¼ cup superfine sugar
1 cinnamon stick
6 cloves
16 allspice berries
4 large cooking pears

■ Place the cider, lemon peel and juice, sugar and spices in a saucepan.
■ Peel the pears, leaving the stems intact, and cut a thin slice from the bottom of each one. Working from the bottom, carefully remove the core from each pear.
■ Bring the poaching liquid to a simmer, add the pears, cover and simmer for about 20 minutes until tender. The timing depends on the ripeness of the pears.
■ Transfer the pears to a serving dish. Bring the liquid to a boil and boil for 5 minutes to reduce slightly. Pour the liquid over the pears and leave to cool, then chill for 2–3 hours or until required.

BURGUNDY PEARS

SERVES 4

≈

½ cup granulated sugar
2 cups red Burgundy wine
pared peel and juice of ½ lemon
2-inch piece of cinnamon stick
4 firm cooking pears
1 tbsp Poire William (pear brandy)

■ Place the sugar, wine, lemon peel and juice and cinnamon in a large saucepan. Simmer gently to dissolve the sugar.
■ Peel the pears carefully, leaving the stems intact, then remove the cores, starting at the bottom of each.
■ Place the pears in the wine and simmer, covered, for about 30 minutes, turning occasionally, until tender. The cooking time will depend on the ripeness of the pears.
■ Transfer the pears and their liquid to a serving dish and leave to go cold. Stir in the Poire William.
■ If wished, the liquid may be strained before serving.

ORCHARD FRUIT COMPOTE

SERVES 4 - 6

≈

2½ cups sugar syrup (*page 60*)
2 pears, peeled, cored and thickly sliced
½ pound plums, halved and pitted
heaped 1 cup gooseberries
heaped 1 cup blackberries

■ Place the sugar syrup in a wide, shallow pan and bring to a simmer.
■ Add the pears and simmer for 5–10 minutes. Add the plums and gooseberries and simmer for a further 5–10 minutes, until all the fruit is just tender. Remove from the heat and add the blackberries.
■ Leave the compote to cool, then chill for 1–2 hours or until required.

TOP *Poached pears in spiced cider;*
BOTTOM *Orchard fruit compote*

POACHED APRICOTS WITH PINE NUTS

S E R V E S   6

≈

Sweetened mascarpone cheese makes a delicious accompaniment to this luxurious fruit dessert. You will find this creamy soft cheese in Italian delicatessens and gourmet food stores.

. . . .

pared peel of 1 orange

pared peel of ½ lemon

2 pounds ripe apricots

2 cups sugar syrup (*see page* 60)

6 tbsp Amaretto (almond liqueur)

2 tbsp pine nuts

. . . .

■ Cut the orange and lemon peels into thin julienne strips. Bring to a boil in cold water, then drain.

■ Place the apricots in a large, shallow dish in a single layer. Pour boiling water over the apricots and leave for 10 seconds. Drain and cover with cold water. Drain once more, then carefully peel off the skins. Cut the fruit in half and discard the pits.

■ Heat the sugar syrup in a large, shallow saucepan, add the apricot halves and the fruit julienne and simmer gently for 5–10 minutes until just tender.

■ Transfer to a serving dish and add the Amaretto. Ensure that the apricots are completely covered with the syrup and chill for 2–3 hours or until required.

■ Roast the pine nuts in a preheated 350°F oven for about 15 minutes. Sprinkle the pine nuts over the apricots just before serving.

STRAWBERRIES IN WINE SYRUP WITH PINK PEPPERCORNS

S E R V E S   4 – 6

≈

Although it may seem odd to combine strawberries with peppercorns, pepper, in fact, brings out the flavor of the fruit. The strawberries should not be marinated for longer than an hour; after this, they begin to lose their color.

. . . .

¼ cup confectioners' sugar

1 tsp pink peppercorns, crushed

⅔ cup Beaumes de Venise dessert wine

1 pound strawberries, washed and hulled

edible flowers such as pansies or borage, to decorate

. . . .

■ Dissolve the sugar in ⅔ cup water, add the peppercorns and bring to a boil. Bubble for 5 minutes, then remove from the heat and add the wine. Leave to cool. Halve or slice the strawberries and add to the syrup.

■ Chill for about 1 hour, then serve decorated with edible flowers.

TOP *Strawberries in wine syrup with pink peppercorns;*
BOTTOM *Poached apricots with pine nuts*

APRICOT DAQUOISE

SERVES 10

≈

The meringue layers may be made in advance and stored in an airtight container until ready for use.

. . . .

MERINGUE LAYERS

½ cup blanched almonds

½ cup brazil nuts

5 egg whites

pinch of salt

I cup superfine sugar

2 tsp cornstarch

APRICOT PUREE

I cup dried apricots, thoroughly washed

generous ¾ cup boiling water

6–7 tbsp orange juice

2 cups heavy cream, whipped

. . . .

▨ Roast all the nuts in a preheated 350°F oven for about 20 minutes until golden, then finely grate or grind them.

▨ Beat the egg whites with a pinch of salt until stiff, then beat in the sugar a spoonful at a time, adding the cornstarch with the last spoonful of sugar. Fold in the nuts.

▨ Using a pastry bag fitted with a ¾-inch tip, pipe two 9-inch circles of the egg-white mixture on foil on a cookie sheet. Start piping from the center and work in one continuous movement.

▨ Bake the meringue circles in a preheated 300°F oven for about I hour. Leave to go cold, then remove the foil.

▨ To make the apricot puree, place the apricots and water in a saucepan, cover and simmer for 15 minutes until tender. Leave to cool, then puree in a blender with enough orange juice to make a thick puree.

▨ Sandwich the 2 meringue layers together with one-third of the cream and most of the apricot puree, reserving about 2 tbsp of the puree for decoration.

▨ Spread the top layer with half of the remaining cream. Put the reserved apricot puree in a small pastry bag fitted with a plain tip and pipe several parallel lines across the cream. Using a skewer, draw lines across the puree in alternate directions to give a feathered effect. Use the remaining cream to pipe a decorative finish around the outside edge of the meringue. Chill until required.

RASPBERRY AND PEAR DAQUOISE

SERVES 10

≈

. . . .

MERINGUE LAYERS

Make the layers as in the recipe for Apricot daquoise (*see left*) but replace the brazil nuts with filberts

FILLING

I cup washed and chopped dried pears

⅔ cup boiling water

2 tbsp granulated sugar

I ½ cups raspberries

. . . .

▨ Place the pears, water, sugar and half the raspberries in a saucepan. Simmer, covered, for 15–20 minutes, until the pears are tender and most of the liquid has been absorbed. Leave to cool.

▨ Reserve 24 whole raspberries, then add the remainder to the pear mixture. Puree in a blender or food processor until smooth and pass through a strainer to remove the seeds, if desired.

▨ Fill and decorate the daquoise with the whipped cream and puree as described in the preceding recipe, then top with the reserved raspberries.

Apricot daquoise

INDIVIDUAL SUMMER FRUIT MOLDS

SERVES 6

≈

For a special occasion, pour a spoonful of fruit liqueur such as Crème de Cassis, Crème de Fraise or Crème de Framboise over these just before serving.

. . . .

1 ½ cups each of black currants, red currants, blackberries, raspberries and strawberries

⅓ cup superfine sugar

12 thin slices of whole-wheat bread, crusts removed

. . . .

▨ Reserve a few berries for decoration, then place the remaining fruit in a saucepan with the sugar. Cook over a gentle heat until all the fruit is soft and there is plenty of liquid.

▨ Use 2 slices of bread to line each of 6 individual molds, cutting and fitting as required. Save the trimmings to make the bottoms.

▨ Spoon the fruit and some liquid into the bread-lined molds and cover with the bread trimmings. Any excess liquid may be spooned on top or reserved and poured over the desserts when they are unmolded.

▨ Cover with plastic wrap and place a light weight on top of each. Chill overnight, then unmold.

▨ To serve, decorate with the reserved berries.

VARIATION

TRADITIONAL SUMMER FRUIT MOLD

To make a large summer fruit mold, cut the bread into fingers and use these to line the sides of a 5-cup mixing bowl, overlapping them as you go. Cut a circle of bread for the bottom and fit it into the bottom of the bowl.

Continue as described in the receipe opposite, filling the bowl generously with the prepared fruit and topping with enough bread to make a firm base.

Cover and lightly weight, then chill overnight. Unmold and serve with raspberry coulis (page 72) and fresh cream. Any combination of summer berries of your choice may be used for this dessert.

Individual summer fruit molds

FRUIT BASKETS WITH BUTTERSCOTCH SAUCE

MAKES 8

≈

....

BASKETS

¼ cup unsalted butter

¼ cup superfine sugar

2 tbsp light corn syrup

½ cup less 1 tbsp all-purpose flour

½ tsp ground ginger

6 ripe peaches, peeled, pits removed
and sliced

⅔ cup blackberries or raspberries

SAUCE

½ cup granulated sugar

⅔ cup water

6 tbsp unsalted butter, diced

1 tsp lemon juice

1¼ cups light cream

....

◼ To make the baskets, melt the butter with the sugar and syrup in a saucepan over a gentle heat. Remove from the heat and stir in the sifted flour and ginger.

◼ Drop tablespoonfuls of the mixture onto well-greased cookie sheets, allowing plenty of space between each. Bake in rotation in a preheated 350°F oven for 7–10 minutes until golden.

◼ Leave to cool for about 1 minute, then loosen from the cookie sheet. Mold the cookies inside small dessert dishes to make the baskets. Leave until completely cold and crisp. Fill the baskets with the prepared fruit and chill while making the sauce.

◼ For the sauce, dissolve the sugar in the water over a gentle heat, then bring to a boil and cook to a strong caramel color. Remove from the heat and stir in the butter and lemon juice. Allow to cool slightly, then stir in the cream and leave to cool.

◼ To serve, place a basket on each plate and pour a little butterscotch sauce around each portion.

FRESH FRUIT PORRIDGE

SERVES 4 – 6

≈

This healthy dessert keeps well in the refrigerator and is also delicious for breakfast or brunch. It is based on oats, which are the most digestible of all the cereals. Lightly stewed fruit may be used as an alternative to fresh fruit.

....

6 tbsp milk

2 tbsp jumbo rolled oats

⅔ cup natural yogurt

2 tbsp soft brown sugar

2 tbsp lemon juice

4 tbsp chopped assorted nuts, toasted

1 pound prepared fruit of your choice, such
as peaches, plums, grapes, bananas, pears
and apples

sprigs of lemon balm or mint, to decorate

....

◼ Warm the milk and soak the rolled oats for 10 minutes, then stir in all the remaining ingredients. Chill for at least 1–2 hours or until required.

◼ Serve in individual dishes decorated with sprigs of lemon balm or mint.

TOP *Fresh fruit porridge;*
BOTTOM *Fruit baskets with butterscotch sauce*

BANANA SOURED CREAM TART

SERVES 8

≈

....

PIECRUST

1 cup all-purpose flour

pinch of salt

6 tbsp unsalted butter

2 tbsp superfine sugar

1 tbsp sesame seeds

2 tsp water

FILLING

¾ cup cream cheese

2 tbsp superfine sugar

4 medium-sized bananas

1 tbsp lemon juice

⅔ cup heavy cream, whipped

GLAZE

1½ tbsp lemon juice

3 tbsp water

3 tbsp confectioners' sugar, sifted

¾ tsp arrowroot

....

▨ Sift together the flour and salt and cut in the butter. Add the remaining ingredients and work to a firm dough. Chill for at least 15 minutes, then roll out on a lightly floured board and use to line a deep-sided 8-inch fluted loose-bottomed tart pan. Chill until firm, then bake blind in a preheated 375°F oven for about 40 minutes until crisp and golden. Leave to go cold.

▨ Beat the cream cheese and sugar together. Mash 2 of the bananas and fold into the mixture with the lemon juice and cream. Spoon into the tart shell.

▨ Combine all the ingredients for the glaze in a small saucepan and bring to a boil, stirring. Cook for 1 minute, then leave to cool slightly.

▨ Peel and slice the remaining bananas and arrange them decoratively over the surface of the pie. Brush with the lemon glaze and chill until required.

▨ This pie is best served fresh on the day it is made.

AVOCADO AND LIME CHIFFON TART

SERVES 8

≈

....

CRUMB CRUST

2 cups crushed gingersnaps

½ cup unsalted butter, melted

FILLING

1 large, ripe avocado, peeled and seed removed

juice of 1 lime

¾ cup confectioners' sugar, sifted

1½ tsp unflavored gelatin

2 tbsp water

⅔ cup heavy cream, lightly whipped

2 egg whites

pinch of salt

....

▨ Mix the cookie crumbs and butter together and use to line the bottom and sides of an 8-inch fluted loose-bottomed tart pan. Bake in a preheated 375°F oven for 15 minutes. Leave to go cold.

▨ Puree the avocado, lime juice and half the sugar in a blender or food processor until smooth. Dissolve the gelatin in the water over a gentle heat and add to the puree. Fold the puree into the whipped cream.

▨ Stiffly beat the egg whites with a pinch of salt, then beat in the remaining sugar a little at a time.

▨ Fold into the avocado mixture and pour into the prepared tart shell. Chill for 3–4 hours or until required.

▨ This pie is best served fresh on the day it is made.

TOP *Avocado and lime chiffon tart;*
BOTTOM *Banana soured cream tart*

TROPICAL GATEAU

SERVES 8

≈

. . . .

CAKE LAYERS

½ cup unsalted butter

½ cup superfine sugar

2 tbsp warm water

2 eggs, beaten

¾ cup self-rising flour

½ tsp baking powder

¾ cup shredded coconut

4 tbsp sugar syrup (*see page* 60)

2 tbsp dark rum

FILLING AND TOPPING

1 pound prepared exotic fruit such as
mango, star fruit, kiwi, orange, pineapple and
grapes

1 cup heavy cream, whipped

¼ cup shredded coconut, toasted

3 tbsp apricot glaze (*see page* 122)

. . . .

▪ Cream together the butter and sugar until pale and fluffy. Beat in the water and eggs a little at a time. Sift together the self-rising flour and baking powder, then fold into the mixture. Fold in the shredded coconut.

▪ Divide the mixture between two 8-inch cake pans and bake in a preheated 350°F oven for about 25 minutes, until risen and firm to the touch. Cool on a wire rack, then transfer to a plastic tray.

▪ Mix the sugar syrup and rum together and drizzle over the cakes until absorbed.

▪ Cut about half the fruit into neat slices and reserve for decorating the top of the cake. Finely chop the remaining fruit and drain off any excess juice.

▪ Fold the chopped fruit into about two-thirds of the whipped cream and use this to sandwich the 2 cake layers together.

▪ Spread the remaining cream over the sides of the cake and coat with the toasted coconut. Arrange the slices of fruit attractively on top of the cake and brush with apricot glaze. Chill until required.

BLACK-CHERRY GATEAU

SERVES 8

≈

. . . .

CAKE LAYERS

Prepare the cake layers as described in the
receipe for Tropical gateau (*see left*)

FILLING AND TOPPING

1-pound can black cherries

1½ tsp unflavored gelatin

1¼ cups heavy cream

¼ cup shredded coconut, toasted

. . . .

▪ Drain the cherries, reserving the juice. Dissolve the gelatin in the juice over a very gentle heat and pour two-thirds of it into a pan to make a shallow layer. Chill until set, then chop into small pieces.

▪ Pit the cherries and reserve. Chill the remaining gelatin liquid until just on the point of setting, then stir in the cherries.

▪ Whip the cream until it just holds its shape and divide into 3 portions. Stir the chopped gelatin into one portion and sandwich the 2 cake layers together with this mixture. Spoon the cherries in the gelatin onto the top of the cake, leaving a ¾-inch rim around the edge of the cake. Spread another portion of the cream onto the sides of the cake and coat with the toasted coconut.

▪ Using a pastry bag fitted with a star tip, pipe the remaining cream decoratively around the top edge of the cake. Chill until required.

Tropical gateau

DEEP-PAN CHEESECAKE

SERVES 10-12

≈

The cream cheese used in this cheesecake gives it a very rich and creamy texture.

. . . .

CRUMB CRUST

1¾ cups crushed graham cracker crumbs

6 tbsp unsalted butter, melted

2 tbsp soft brown sugar

1 tsp ground cinnamon

FILLING AND TOPPING

3 cups cream cheese

4 eggs

6 tbsp superfine sugar

finely grated peel and juice of 1 large lemon

2 tbsp all-purpose flour, sifted

2 cups soured cream

3 tbsp superfine sugar

½ tsp vanilla essence

. . . .

▨ Combine the ingredients for the crust and press onto the bottom of an 8-inch springform pan. Butter the sides of the pan. Chill until required.

▨ Beat together the cream cheese, eggs, superfine sugar, lemon peel and juice and the flour and pour onto the crumb crust.

▨ Bake in a preheated 375°F oven for about 50 minutes until just set. Remove from the oven and cool slightly.

▨ Beat together the remaining ingredients and carefully pour on top of the cheesecake. Return to the oven for 5 minutes. Switch off the oven and leave the cake to cool in the oven.

▨ Chill the cheesecake for at least 12 hours before unmolding and serving.

INDIVIDUAL PASHKAS

SERVES 6

≈

. . . .

1½ cups curd cheese

1 egg yolk

6 tbsp soured cream

¼ cup unsalted butter

3 tbsp superfine sugar

2 tbsp raisins

⅓ cup finely chopped assorted candied fruit

2 tbsp toasted and chopped
blanched almonds

1 tsp rosewater

small pieces of candied fruit, to decorate

plain cookies, to serve

. . . .

▨ Wrap the curd cheese in a piece of cheesecloth, then place in a colander and leave to drain, preferably overnight.

▨ Beat the cheese, egg yolk and soured cream together. Beat the butter and sugar until pale and fluffy and stir in the cheese mixture until evenly combined. Stir in the remaining ingredients.

▨ Line 6 individual dariole molds with cheesecloth and press the mixture into each one. Fold the cheesecloth over the top of each mixture and invert the molds onto a wire tray set over a plastic tray. Chill overnight.

▨ Unmold onto individual serving dishes and decorate with small pieces of candied fruit. Serve with plain cookies.

TOP *Deep-pan cheesecake;*

BOTTOM *Individual pashka*

ORANGE ROULADE

SERVES 8

≈

. . . .

4 eggs, separated

½ cup superfine sugar

finely grated peel of 2 medium-sized oranges

juice of ½ medium-sized orange

½ cup plus 1 tbsp finely ground bleached almonds

1 tbsp all-purpose flour, sifted

⅔ cup heavy cream

1 tbsp Grand Marnier

fresh rosebuds, to decorate (optional)

. . . .

▨ Beat the egg yolks and 6 tbsp of the sugar with the orange peel and juice until thick and pale.

▨ Beat the egg whites until stiff, then beat in the remaining sugar.

▨ Fold 2 heaped tbsp of the ground almonds and the flour into the egg-yolk mixture alternately with the egg whites.

▨ Transfer the mixture to a 13- × 9-inch pan lined with waxed paper and bake in a preheated 350°F oven for about 25 minutes, until just firm to the touch.

▨ Place a sheet of waxed paper on one side of a dampened dish towel, sprinkle it with the remaining ground almonds and invert the cooked cake onto the paper. Cover with the other half of the dish towel and leave to go cold. Remove the lining paper.

▨ Whip the double cream with the Grand Marnier until stiff, then spread it over the cake in an even layer. Starting at a short end, roll up the cake to make a neat roll.

▨ Trim the edges to neaten them and serve decorated with fresh rosebuds, if desired.

VARIATIONS

LEMON ROULADE

Replace the orange peel and juice in the recipe with the finely grated peel of 2 lemons and the juice of 1 lemon. Follow the method described in the recipe. Fill with ⅔ cup heavy cream whipped with 1 tbsp sifted confectioners' sugar. Dust with confectioners' sugar before serving and decorate with rosebuds, if desired.

COFFEE ROULADE

Omit the orange peel and juice in the recipe and replace with 1 tbsp instant coffee dissolved in 3 tbsp boiling water. Follow the method described in the recipe. Fill with ⅔ cup whipped heavy cream flavored with 1 tbsp coffee or chocolate liqueur and 1 tbsp sifted confectioners' sugar. Decorate with chocolate leaves (see page 10), if desired.

Orange roulade

PINEAPPLE FROMAGE FRAIS CAKE

SERVES 10

≈

. . . .

2 egg whites

pinch of salt

½ cup superfine sugar

I medium-sized pineapple weighing about
2½ pounds, peeled, cored and chopped

⅔ cup sugar syrup (*see page* 60)

2 tbsp unflavored gelatin

6 tbsp water

I cup cream cheese

2 cups fromage frais

I cup heavy cream, whipped

TO DECORATE

fresh pineapple pieces (optional)

lemon-balm leaves (optional)

. . . .

▨ Draw an 8-inch circle on a piece of foil on a cookie sheet. Beat the egg whites with a pinch of salt until stiff, then beat in the sugar a little at a time until thick and glossy. Spoon or pipe the meringue onto the cookie sheet following the outline of the circle. Level the surface and bake in a preheated 300°F oven for 1½ hours until crisp.

▨ Line the bottom and sides of an 8-inch springform pan with waxed paper. Press the meringue disc onto the bottom of the pan, trimming it as necessary.

▨ Place the pineapple and sugar syrup in a saucepan and bring to a boil. Simmer for 5 minutes, then drain well, reserving the syrup. Leave to cool, then puree half the pineapple with the syrup.

▨ Dissolve the gelatin in the water and stir into the pineapple puree. Beat in the cream cheese and fromage frais, then fold in the chopped pineapple. Transfer the mixture to the prepared pan and level the surface. Chill for 6–8 hours, or preferably overnight, until set.

▨ Unmold the cake onto a serving plate. Pipe the cream around the edge and decorate as desired.

INDIVIDUAL PAVLOVA NESTS

MAKES 6

≈

These small Pavlova nests are much easier to handle and serve than the traditional large one.

. . . .

4 egg whites

pinch of salt

I cup plus I tbsp superfine sugar

2 tsp arrowroot or cornstarch

I tsp vinegar

I tsp vanilla essence

I small mango

2 tangerines

¼ pineapple

½ papaya

2 passion fruit

1¼ cups heavy cream, whipped

2 tbsp toasted and chopped
macadamia nuts

. . . .

▨ Draw six 4-inch circles on a large sheet of foil placed on a cookie sheet.

▨ Beat the egg whites and salt until stiff, then beat in the sugar a little at a time until thick and glossy. Mix the arrowroot with the last spoonful of sugar and beat into the mixture. Fold in the vinegar and vanilla essence.

▨ Divide the mixture between the 6 prepared circles and shape into nests.

▨ Bake in a preheated 300°F oven for 1 hour. Leave to go cold on the cookie sheet.

▨ Prepare all the fruit and cut as required. Divide the cream between the nests and top with the fruit and macadamia nuts.

▨ Chill for about 1 hour before serving.

TOP *Individual Pavlova nests;*
BOTTOM *Pineapple fromage frais cake*

TIRAMESU

SERVES 10

≈

This outstanding version of a delicious traditional Italian tipsy cake is literally soaked with brandy and coffee liqueur.

. . . .

I cup freshly made black coffee

¼ cup brandy

¼ cup coffee liqueur

2 tbsp superfine sugar or soft brown sugar

¾ pound Madeira cake

I pound mascarpone cheese

TO DECORATE

whipped cream

sugared coffee beans

. . . .

■ Line the bottom and sides of a 7-inch springform pan with waxed paper. An 8-inch pan may be used, however the cake will be thinner.

■ Combine the coffee, brandy, coffee liqueur and sugar.

■ Cut the Madeira cake into thin slices and, using about one-third of the cake, cover the bottom of the pan completely, cutting and fitting as necessary. Soak the cake with about one-third of the coffee liquid.

■ Beat the mascarpone cheese until smooth and spread half on top of the first layer of cake. Repeat the layering until all the ingredients have been used up. Cover and chill the cake for 4–6 hours or until required.

■ Unmold the cake onto a serving place. Pipe rosettes of whipped cream on top and decorate with sugared coffee beans.

TIRAMESU "TRIFLE"

SERVES 6 – 8

≈

In this version of Tiramesu, the mascarpone cheese is lightened by the addition of eggs and the mixture is prepared in a serving dish. This dessert may be assembled and served in individual dishes rather than in one large dish as suggested here.

. . . .

10 ounces mascarpone cheese

2 eggs separated

¼ cup superfine sugar

8–12 ladyfingers, halved

approx. ⅔ cup freshly made, strong black coffee

cocoa powder, for dusting

. . . .

■ Beat the mascarpone cheese with the egg yolks until smooth. Beat the egg whites until stiff, then beat in the sugar a spoonful at a time until the mixture is thick and glossy. Fold this into the cheese mixture.

■ Dip the ladyfingers in the coffee until well soaked, then arrange in the bottom of a serving dish. Cover with the cheese mixture and chill for at least 6 hours, or preferably overnight.

■ Place some cocoa powder in a sifter and dust the top of the dessert generously. Serve at once.

Tiramesu

RHUBARB AND STRAWBERRY CRUNCH PARFAITS

MAKES 4

≈

The amount of crunch mixture below is sufficient for 4 recipe quantities: reserve the unused mixture in an airtight container for other recipes – it makes a popular topping for all sorts of creamy desserts and ice creams.

. . . .

CRUNCH MIXTURE

1 cup jumbo rolled oats

¼ cup light brown sugar

¼ cup slivered almonds

¼ cup shredded coconut

2 tbsp wheatgerm

1 tbsp sunflower seeds

1 tbsp sesame seeds

3 tbsp vegetable oil

2 tbsp water

pinch of salt

few drops of vanilla essence

FRUIT LAYER

1¾ cups sliced rhubarb

¼ cup granulated sugar

½ tsp arrowroot

⅔ cup hulled and quartered strawberries

CREAM LAYER

⅔ cup heavy cream, whipped

⅔ cup natural yogurt

. . . .

▨ To make the crunch mixture, combine all the dry ingredients in a bowl. Mix the remaining ingredients and stir into the bowl. Spread the mixture on a cookie sheet and bake in a preheated 375°F oven for about 30 minutes until golden. Leave to go cold. Use one-quarter of the mixture for this recipe and store the remainder in an airtight container.

▨ Cook the rhubarb and sugar together over a gentle heat until tender – about 15 minutes. Strain the fruit, reserving the juice, and beat the arrowroot into the juice. Cook over a medium heat, stirring all the time until the mixture thickens. Add to the rhubarb and leave to cool. Stir in the strawberries.

▨ Combine the cream and yogurt for the cream layer.

▨ Layer the 3 mixtures in individual glasses: spoon the fruit in first, then the cream and finally the crunch mixture. Repeat the layering at least once more. Chill for at least 1 hour or until required.

ROSEMARY CRÈME BRULÉES

SERVES 6

≈

. . . .

2 × 4-inch sprigs of fresh rosemary

2½ cups heavy cream

5 egg yolks

2 tbsp superfine sugar

6 tbsp confectioners' sugar, sifted

. . . .

▨ Place the sprigs of rosemary and the cream in a saucepan and bring just to a boil. Cook over the very gentlest heat for 5 minutes, then remove from the heat and leave to infuse for 1 hour.

▨ Beat together the egg yolks and sugar and stir in the cream. Strain the custard into 6 ramekin dishes and place these in a roasting pan. Pour in boiling water to come a good halfway up the sides of the ramekin dishes.

▨ Cook in a preheated 250°F oven for about 40 minutes until set. Leave to go cold, then chill for several hours.

▨ Just before serving, cover each custard with an even layer of confectioners' sugar and place under a preheated broiler until the sugar caramelizes. Leave to set.

TOP *Rhubarb and strawberry crunch parfaits;*
BOTTOM *Rosemary crème brulées*

ALMOND AND PASSION FRUIT GATEAU

SERVES 10

≈

7 eggs, separated

1½ cups superfine sugar

¼ cup all-purpose flour

pinch of salt

1½ tsp baking powder

2 tsp ground cinnamon

1 tsp ground ginger

2¾ cups finely grated carrots

1 tsp lemon juice

3 cups finely ground blanched almonds

2 cups heavy cream

2 tbsp confectioners' sugar, sifted

strained juice of 4 passion fruit

⅔ cup slivered almonds, toasted

4 ounces store-bought white marzipan

◾ Beat the egg yolks with three-quarters of the sugar until thick. Sift together the flour, salt, baking powder and spices and fold into the mixture with the carrots and lemon juice. Beat the egg whites until stiff, then gradually beat in the remaining sugar. Fold into the carrot mixture alternately with the ground almonds.

◾ Transfer to a greased and lined 9½-inch springform pan and bake in a preheated 400°F oven for 15 minutes. Reduce the temperature to 350°F and bake for a further 40–45 minutes. Cool in the pan, then transfer to a wire rack and leave until completely cold. Cut into 3 layers.

◾ Whip the cream with the sugar and fold in the passion-fruit juice. Use about half the cream to sandwich the 3 cake layers together, then coat the sides and top of the cake with the remaining cream.

◾ Press the toasted almonds onto the sides of the cake.

◾ Roll out the marzipan thinly and cut out 10 leaf shapes, each about 5 inches long. Mark veins in each leaf, then arrange on top of the gateau. Chill.

SPICED APPLE GATEAU

SERVES 10

≈

7 eggs, separated

1½ cups superfine sugar

⅓ cup less 1 tbsp whole-wheat flour

pinch of salt

1½ tsp baking powder

2 tsp ground cinnamon

3⅓ cups cored and coarsely grated eating apples

1 tsp lemon juice

3 cups finely ground blanched almonds

2½ cups heavy cream

8 tbsp apple juice concentrate

⅔ cup slivered almonds, toasted

1 small apple, cored and thinly sliced

1 tsp lemon juice

◾ Beat the egg yolks with three-quarters of the sugar until thick and pale. Mix together the dry ingredients and fold into the mixture with the grated apples and lemon juice.

◾ Beat the egg whites until stiff, then gradually beat in the remaining sugar. Fold into the apple mixture alternately with the ground almonds.

◾ Transfer to a 9½-inch springform pan. Bake in a preheated 400°F oven for 15 minutes and at 350°F for a further 40–45 minutes. Cool in the pan, then transfer to a wire rack and leave until completely cold. Cut into 3 layers.

◾ Whip the cream lightly, then fold in the apple-juice concentrate. Use about half the cream to sandwich the cake layers together and to coat the sides of the assembled cake. Press the almonds onto the sides. Use the remaining cream to cover and decorate the top of the cake.

◾ Just before serving, toss the apple slices in the lemon juice and arrange on the top of the cake.

Almond and passion fruit gateau

OLD–ENGLISH SHERRY TRIFLE

SERVES 10-12

≈

There are many variations of this typical British dessert. The English usually flavor it with sherry, while the Scots and Irish prefer whisky or white wine.

. . . .

2 eggs

3 egg yolks

¼ cup superfine sugar

1¼ cups milk

2 cups light cream

vanilla bean, split *or* 1 fresh bay leaf

6 slices of pound cake

4 tbsp strawberry or raspberry jam

⅔ cup medium-dry sherry

1½ cups sliced strawberries, or raspberries

2 bananas, sliced

1 cup very roughly crumbled macaroons

2½ cups heavy cream, lightly whipped

TO DECORATE

candied violets

candied rose petals

toasted slivered almonds

. . . .

▓ Beat together the eggs, egg yolks and sugar.

▓ Place the milk, cream and vanilla bean in a saucepan and bring just to a boil. Leave to infuse for 5 minutes, then pour onto the eggs and combine thoroughly.

▓ Cook the custard in a heatproof bowl set over a saucepan of simmering water until it has thickened enough to coat the back of a wooden spoon. Alternatively, cook in a microwave oven on a medium-high setting for about 6 minutes, stirring every 30 seconds. Strain and leave to cool.

▓ Split the cake slices and sandwich together with the jam. Cut each cake sandwich into 3 pieces and place in a single layer on the bottom of a large glass serving dish.

▓ Cover with the sherry, then top with a layer of the fruit, followed by the macaroons. Pour the custard on top, cover and leave to cool. Chill the trifle for 3–4 hours until set.

▓ Top with the whipped cream and decorate with candied violets, rose petals and slivered almonds.

GINGER TRIFLE

SERVES 10-12

≈

. . . .

CUSTARD

Follow the recipe for Old-English sherry trifle (*see left*)

6 slices of pound cake

5 tbsp ginger conserve

⅔ cup medium-dry sherry or ginger wine

1 cup very roughly crumbled macaroons

1¼ cups heavy cream

2 tbsp preserved ginger syrup

TO DECORATE

1 tbsp finely chopped preserved ginger

2 tbsp slivered almonds, toasted

. . . .

▓ Make the custard.

▓ Split the cake slices and sandwich together with the ginger conserve. Cut each one into 3 pieces and place in the bottom of a large glass serving dish.

▓ Cover with the sherry, then the macaroons and pour the custard on top. Cover and chill until set.

▓ Whip the cream with the ginger syrup until it holds its shape, then spoon it on top of the custard.

▓ Decorate the top of the trifle with the stem ginger and slivered almonds.

Old-English sherry trifle

ROOM TEMPERATURE

Pastries that form a shell for all sorts of fillings comprise a major part of this chapter. Since the making of a good piecrust or pastry can be tricky, make sure you follow the recipes in this chapter very carefully: they have all been precisely calculated and thoroughly tested.

Pastries are always best eaten fresh on the day they are made; once cooked they should be removed from the oven and left to cool to room temperature before serving. Any leftovers may subsequently be warmed in the oven.

Yeast and other cakes which incorporate syrup are also included in this section. These are best soaked with syrup the minute they come out of the oven, then left to cool to room temperature and served straightaway.

However, if you wish to make them in advance, you can freeze them before adding the syrup. Once thawed, refresh the cakes in the oven to warm them, then soak immediately with the syrup, which will then be more easily absorbed.

CONTENTS

PISTACHIO CONES

MAKES 12

≈

....

¼ cup shelled pistachio nuts

½ cup confectioners' sugar, sifted

2 tbsp unsalted butter, melted

2 tbsp heavy cream

2 tbsp egg white

I tbsp brandy

pinch of salt

2 tbsp all-purpose flour, sifted

TO DECORATE

I ¼ cups heavy cream, whipped

3 dark grapes, quartered and seeds removed

3 green grapes, quartered and seeds removed

I tbsp chopped pistachio nuts

....

▨ Finely grate or grind the pistachio nuts, then mix with the confectioners' sugar. Place all the ingredients in a bowl and mix until thoroughly incorporated. Leave to stand for 30 minutes.

▨ Drop tablespoonfuls of the mixture well apart on greased cookie sheets and bake in a preheated 375°F oven for about 8 minutes, until the cookies are golden at the edges. (In order to get the timing right, place 2 cookies at a time on each cookie sheet, and put the trays in the oven at approximately 5-minute intervals.) Loosen the cookies from the sheets and immediately wrap them around pastry-horn molds. Leave to cool on a wire rack.

▨ When the cones are crisp, carefully twist them off the pastry-horn molds. Store in an airtight container until required.

▨ Just before serving, pipe whipped cream into the cones and decorate with grape quarters and chopped pistachio nuts. If wished, extra chopped grapes may be added to the whipped cream used to fill the cones.

MERINGUE CUPS WITH RED FRUIT

MAKES 12

≈

....

4 egg whites

pinch of salt

heaped ½ cup superfine sugar

I cup confectioners' sugar, sifted

I tbsp cornstarch or arrowroot, sifted

I ¼ cups heavy cream, whipped, or fromage frais

½ pound summer berries such as raspberries, strawberries, black currants and blackberries

12 cherries, with stems and pits removed

12 sprigs of red currants

....

▨ Draw twelve 2½-inch circles on a large sheet of foil and place it on a cookie sheet.

▨ Beat the egg whites and salt until stiff, then beat in the superfine sugar a spoonful at a time. Beat in most of the confectioners' sugar a spoonful at a time, then mix the cornstarch with the remaining sugar and beat into the mixture. The egg-white mixture should be really stiff and glossy at this stage.

▨ Use the egg-white mixture to fill a pastry bag fitted with a ⅜-inch plain tip and pipe meringue cups by following the outlines on the prepared paper. Start in the center of each circle and pipe in a continuous flowing movement until you reach the outside edge, then continue to pipe around the outside edge, building up a wall with 4 or 5 circles.

▨ Bake the meringue cups in a preheated 200°F oven for about 1½ hours until crisp and dry. Leave to go cold on the cookie sheets.

▨ Fill with whipped cream or fromage frais and arrange the fruit on top just before serving.

TOP *Meringue cups with red fruit;*
BOTTOM *Pistachio cones*

LEMON AND LIME MERINGUE TART

SERVES 10

≈

....

PIECRUST

1½ cups all-purpose flour

1 cup finely crushed graham cracker crumbs

heaped ¾ cup unsalted butter

¼ cup superfine sugar

FILLING

finely grated peel and juice of 2 medium-sized lemons

finely grated peel and juice of 1 lime

water

5 tbsp cornstarch

heaped ¾ cup superfine sugar

3 egg yolks

2 tbsp unsalted butter

MERINGUE

3 egg whites

pinch of salt

heaped ¾ cup superfine sugar

....

■ Combine the flour and cracker crumbs, then cut in the butter. Add the sugar and bring together to form a firm dough. Use to line a 10-inch fluted loose-bottomed tart pan. Bake blind in a preheated 350°F oven for about 40 minutes. Leave to go cold.

■ Combine the fruit juices and make up to 2 cups with water. Mix the cornstarch and sugar with a little fruit liquid until smooth. Stir in the remaining liquid and the fruit peels. Bring to the boil, stirring continuously until the mixture thickens. Remove from the heat and stir in the egg yolks, one at a time, then the butter. Pour into the tart shell and leave to cool.

■ Beat the egg whites with a pinch of salt until stiff, then beat in the sugar a spoonful at a time.

■ Cover the surface of the tart with the meringue and bake in a preheated 350°F oven for 20 minutes until golden. Leave to go cold in the pan.

BANANA, RUM AND COCONUT TART

SERVES 10

≈

....

PIECRUST

¾ cup plus 1 tbsp all-purpose flour, sifted

¾ cup whole-wheat flour

6 tbsp cream cheese

6 tbsp unsalted butter

FILLING

¼ cup unsalted butter, melted

2 eggs, beaten

2½ tbsp maple syrup or corn syrup

2 tbsp dark rum

¾ cup shredded coconut

2 ripe bananas sliced

....

■ Combine all the ingredients for the piecrust in a bowl and work to a soft dough. Chill until firm, then press into a 9½-inch fluted loose-bottom tart pan to evenly cover the base and sides. Chill until required.

■ Mix together the butter, eggs, maple syrup, rum and coconut and fold in the banana slices.

■ Transfer the filling to the tart shell and bake in a preheated 350°F oven for 45 minutes until the filling has set. Leave to go cold in the pan.

TOP *Banana, rum and coconut tart;*

BOTTOM *Lemon and lime meringue tart*

PEAR AND FRANGIPANE TARTLETTES

MAKES 6

≈

....

PIECRUST

1½ cups all-purpose flour

½ cup unsalted butter

2 tbsp superfine sugar

1 tbsp cold water

FRANGIPANE AND PEAR FILLING

¼ cup unsalted butter

¼ cup superfine sugar

1 egg

½ cup finely ground blanched almonds

1 tbsp all-purpose flour

1 tbsp lemon juice

2 ounces store-bought marzipan, diced

3 small pears

1 tbsp lemon juice

apricot glaze (*see page* 122)

....

▧ Sift the flour into a bowl, cut in the butter, stir in the sugar and mix to a firm dough with the water. Roll out on a lightly floured board and use to line six 4-inch fluted loose-bottomed tartlette pans. Chill until required.

▧ To make the frangipane, beat the butter with the sugar until pale and fluffy. Beat in the egg, then fold in the ground almonds and flour. Stir in the lemon juice and finally the diced marzipan.

▧ Divide the mixture between the tart shells and spread evenly.

▧ Peel the pears and cut in half lengthwise. Carefully remove the cores and cut almost through each pear-half in a series of lines to give a decorative pattern. Brush each pear with lemon juice as it is prepared.

▧ Place a pear-half in the center of each tartlette, then bake in a preheated 375°F oven for about 30 minutes until golden.

▧ Leave to cool, then brush the surface of each tartlette with apricot glaze.

FRENCH LEMON PIE

SERVES 10

≈

....

PIECRUST

1¾ cups all-purpose flour

⅔ cup unsalted butter

2½ tbsp superfine sugar

4 tsp water

FILLING

6 tbsp superfine sugar

3 eggs

finely grated peel and juice of 3 large lemons

½ cup finely ground blanched almonds

6 tbsp unsalted butter, melted

whipped cream, to decorate

....

▧ Sift the flour into a bowl, cut in the butter and stir in the sugar. Add the water and work to a firm dough. Reserve about one sixth of the dough to make the leaf decorations. Roll out the remaining dough and use to line a 9½-inch pie plate with a wide rim. Bake blind in a preheated 375°F oven for 30 minutes, then leave to cool.

▧ Roll out the reserved dough trimmings thinly and stamp out as many small leaf shapes as possible. Mark the veins on each one with a small knife.

▧ To make the filling, beat together the sugar, eggs and lemon peel and juice, then stir in the ground almonds and melted butter.

▧ Pour the filling into the partially baked pie shell and press the leaves onto the edge of the pie in a random pattern.

▧ Bake in a preheated 375°F oven for a further 30 minutes until the filling has set and the leaves are golden. Leave to cool to room temperature.

▧ Pipe a border of whipped cream around the pie just before serving.

TOP *Pear and frangipane tartlettes;*
BOTTOM *French lemon pie*

GRAPE TART

SERVES 8

≈

....

PIECRUST

1¼ cups all-purpose flour, sifted

¼ cup superfine sugar

6 tbsp butter

I egg yolk

FILLING

I cup cream cheese

5 tbsp white grape juice

I egg, separated

2 tbsp all-purpose flour, sifted

¼ cup superfine sugar

finely grated peel of I lemon

TOPPING

4 ounces small seedless grapes, halved

1½ tsp arrowroot

½ cup white grape juice

I fresh grape leaf or other edible leaf

....

■ Mix the flour and sugar in a bowl, then cut in the butter. Mix to a firm dough with the egg yolk. Use to line a deep-sided 8-inch fluted loose bottomed tart pan. Chill until firm, then bake blind in a preheated 375°F oven for 30 minutes.

■ Meanwhile, beat together the cream cheese, grape juice, egg yolk, flour, half the sugar and the lemon peel. Beat the egg white until stiff and beat in the remaining sugar a little at a time. Fold into the cheese mixture and transfer to the cooled tart shell.

■ Bake for a further 30 minutes in a preheated 350°F oven. Leave to cool to room temperature When the filling has set, arrange the grapes to look like a bunch on top of the tart.

■ Mix the arrowroot with the grape juice and bring to a boil in a small saucepan. Simmer for 1–2 minutes, stirring constantly. Leave to cool slightly.

■ Arrange a grape leaf on the surface of the tart and brush the glaze over the whole surface. Leave to cool.

NECTARINE-TOPPED FUDGE TART

SERVES 10

≈

....

CRUMB CRUST

1¾ cups finely crushed graham cracker crumbs

6 tbsp unsalted butter, melted

FILLING

1¾ cups condensed milk

¾ cup unsalted butter

¾ cup soft brown sugar

I tbsp lemon juice

2–3 nectarines, thinly sliced, to decorate

....

■ Combine the cracker crumbs and butter and use to line the bottom and sides of a deep 8-inch fluted loose-bottomed tart pan. Bake in a preheated 350°F oven for 15 minutes.

■ Place the condensed milk, butter, sugar and lemon juice in a large, heavy-bottomed saucepan and cook over the gentlest heat, stirring all the time until the sugar dissolves. Continue cooking, stirring constantly until the mixture is a rich, fudge color. Pour into the prepared tart shell and leave to go cold in the pan.

■ Unmold the tart onto a serving plate and decorate with the nectarine slices.

TOP *Nectarine-topped fudge tart;*
BOTTOM *Grape tart*

PUMPKIN CHEESE TART

SERVES 8

≈

A good way to prepare and cook pumpkin is to cut it into wedges weighing about 1 pound each and to remove the seeds. Bake it in a preheated 350°F oven for about 45 minutes until just tender. It can then be peeled and diced ready for use. Cooked pumpkin also freezes well.

PIECRUST

1 cup plus 1 tbsp all-purpose flour

pinch of salt

6 tbsp unsalted butter

2 tbsp superfine sugar

2 tsp cold water

FILLING

4 ounces cooked pumpkin

¼ cup superfine sugar

finely grated peel and juice of ½ lemon

½ cup cream cheese

4 tbsp heavy cream

2 tbsp all-purpose flour, sifted

⅛ tsp ground nutmeg

2 eggs, separated

▪ To make the dough, combine the flour and salt and cut in the butter. Stir in the sugar and work to a firm dough with the water. Roll out on a lightly floured board and use to line a deep-sided 8-inch fluted loose-bottomed tart pan. Chill until firm, then bake blind in a preheated 375°F oven for 20 minutes.

▪ Meanwhile, puree all the ingredients except the egg whites in a blender or food processor until smooth. Stiffly beat the egg whites, then fold into the pumpkin mixture.

▪ Pour the filling into the partially baked tart shell and bake in a preheated 325°F oven for a further 30–40 minutes until just set. Leave to cool to room temperature.

APPLE TART

SERVES 8

≈

PIECRUST

¾ cup shelled filberts

6 tbsp unsalted butter

¼ cup superfine sugar

1 cup whole-wheat flour

1 tbsp poppy seeds

pinch of salt

FILLING

2 pounds eating apples, pared, cored and sliced

finely grated peel of 1 lemon

2 tbsp apricot jam

2 tbsp candied peel, finely chopped

4 tbsp golden raisins

4 tbsp dried currants

apricot glaze (*see page* 122)

▪ To make the dough, finely chop or grate the filberts. Cream together the butter and sugar until pale and fluffy, then mix in the remaining ingredients and work to a dough. Chill for 30 minutes. Use the dough to line the bottom and sides of a deep-sided 8-inch fluted tart pan.

▪ To make the filling, place the apple slices, lemon peel and jam in a wide, shallow saucepan. Cover and cook over a gentle heat for about 5 minutes, until just tender, shaking the pan frequently to prevent the apple slices from sticking to the bottom. Add the candied peel, golden raisins and currants, then cool before using to fill the tart shell.

▪ Bake in a preheated 375°F oven for 50 minutes. Brush the surface of the apples with a little apricot glaze and leave to cool to room temperature before serving.

TOP *Pumpkin cheese tart;*
BOTTOM *Apple tart*

APPLE, BLACKBERRY AND FRANGIPANE JALOUSIE

SERVES 6-8

≈

PASTRY

I cup unsalted butter

3 cups all-purpose flour

pinch of salt

¼ cup superfine sugar

2 tbsp cold water

FILLING AND TOPPING

¼ cup unsalted butter

¼ cup superfine sugar

I egg, beaten

½ cup finely ground blanched almonds

I tbsp all-purpose flour, sifted

3 eating apples, pared, cored and quartered

4 ounces blackberries

beaten egg white, to glaze

I tbsp granulated sugar

■ Cut the butter into the flour and salt. Stir in the superfine sugar and mix to a firm dough with the water.

■ To make the frangipane, beat the butter and sugar together until pale and fluffy. Beat in the egg, then fold in the ground almonds and flour.

■ Roll the dough out on a lightly floured board to a 12- × 10-inch oblong. Cut in half lengthwise and place one half on a cookie sheet. Spread the frangipane to within ½ inch of the edge and arrange the fruit on top. Brush the edges with beaten egg white. Make small slashes in the second piece of dough and lay this on the fruit, pressing it well at the edges to seal. Crimp the edges to give a decorative finish.

■ Brush the surface of the dough with egg white and sprinkle with the granulated sugar. Bake in a preheated 375°F oven for about 50 minutes until golden. Leave to cool to room temperature.

■ This dessert is best served on the day it is made

BLUEBERRY SHORTBREADS

MAKES 8

≈

I ½ cups all-purpose flour

pinch of salt

½ cup unsalted butter

¾ cup finely ground blanched almonds

6 tbsp superfine sugar

I egg yolk

TO DECORATE

heavy cream, lightly whipped

fresh blueberries

■ Sift together the flour and salt and cut in the butter. Add the ground almonds and sugar and work the mixture to a dough with the egg yolk.

■ Roll the dough out on a lightly floured board to about ½ inch thickness and stamp out eight 3-inch circles. Use the trimmings to make 16 leaves and mark the veins with a small knife.

■ Place the circles on a cookie sheet and attach 2 leaves to each using a drop of water. Bake in a preheated 325°F oven for about 30 minutes until golden. Cool on a wire rack.

■ Top each shortbread with cream and some fresh blueberries just before serving.

TOP *Blueberry shortbreads;*
BOTTOM *Apple, blackberry and frangipane jalousie*

RED CURRANT SAVARIN

SERVES 8 – 10

≈

. . . .

2 cups hard all-purpose or bread flour, sifted

½ tsp salt

¼ cup superfine sugar

1 tbsp rapid-rise dried yeast

6 tbsp milk

4 eggs, beaten

½ cup unsalted butter, softened

½ pound red currants

SYRUP

⅔ cup granulated sugar

1 cup water

5 tbsp dark rum

apricot glaze (*see right*)

sprig of red currants, to decorate

. . . .

▦ Sift the flour, salt and sugar into a bowl and make a well in the center. Sprinkle the yeast into the well. Warm the milk until just tepid and pour into the well. Cover and leave to froth for about 15 minutes.

▦ Add the eggs and butter and beat well until evenly mixed. Stir in the red currants.

▦ Transfer the mixture to a greased and floured 8-inch springform pan. Cover and leave to rise in a warm place for about 1 hour, until the mixture reaches almost to the top of the pan.

▦ Bake in a preheated 350°F oven for about 40 minutes until risen and firm to the touch. Unmold onto a wire rack placed over a tray.

▦ To make the syrup, dissolve the sugar in the water over a gentle heat. Bring to a boil and boil for 3 minutes. Remove from the heat and stir in the rum. Spoon over the savarin until completely absorbed.

▦ Brush the surface of the savarin with apricot glaze and decorate with a sprig of red currants.

▦ The savarin is best if served fresh on the day it is made.

VARIATIONS

The red currants in this recipe can be replaced with any other berries such as black currants, blueberries, blackberries or strawberries.

APRICOT GLAZE

MAKES 1 CUP

≈

Apricot glaze can be made and stored in a refrigerator for several weeks. Warm it gently in a saucepan or microwave oven when required.

. . . .

¾ cup apricot jam

2 tbsp water

dash of lemon juice

. . . .

▦ Place the ingredients in a saucepan and heat gently until the jam has melted, then boil for 1 minute. Strain, cool and use as required.

Red currant savarin

DATE AND ORANGE TORTE

SERVES 8

≈

· ·

⅓ cup all-purpose flour

I tsp baking powder

¼ tsp salt

3 eggs, separated

6 tbsp soft brown sugar

4 tbsp vegetable oil

finely grated peel of I medium-sized orange

I cup chopped dates

I cup roughly chopped walnuts

juice of I medium-sized orange

3 tbsp confectioners' sugar

12 kumquats, sliced

⅔ cup sugar syrup (*see page* 60)

whipped cream

· ·

▪ Sift together the flour, baking powder and salt. Beat the egg yolks with the sugar until thick and pale. Beat in the oil and orange peel. Stiffly beat the egg whites. Fold the flour mixture, dates and walnuts into the egg-yolk mixture alternately with the egg whites until evenly combined.

▪ Transfer to a greased and lined 9-inch springform pan. Bake in a preheated 350°F oven for about 30 minutes until risen and firm to the touch.

▪ Place the orange juice and confectioners' sugar in a saucepan and bring to a boil. Pour over the warm cake and leave to cool in the pan.

▪ Cook the kumquat slices in the syrup for about 5 minutes until tender. Leave to go cold. Drain and reserve a few slices for decoration. Place the remainder in a separate bowl.

▪ Pipe a little whipped cream on top of the torte and decorate with kumquat slices. Serve the reserved kumquat slices as an accompaniment to the torte.

SPICED PRUNE AND ALMOND TORTE

SERVES 8

≈

· ·

⅓ cup whole-wheat flour

I tsp baking powder

½ tsp baking soda

¼ tsp salt

I tsp apple pie spice

3 eggs, separated

½ cup soft brown sugar

4 tbsp vegetable oil

½ cup buttermilk

⅔ cup chopped prunes

½ cup finely ground blanched almonds

GLAZE

3 tbsp maple syrup or honey

3 tbsp buttermilk

TO DECORATE

whipped cream

toasted slivered almonds

· ·

▪ Mix together the flour, baking powder, baking soda, salt and apple pie spice.

▪ Beat the egg yolks with the sugar until thick and pale, then stir in the oil and buttermilk. Stir in the prunes and ground almonds. Stiffly beat the egg whites and fold into the mixture.

▪ Transfer the mixture to a greased 9-inch springform pan lined on the bottom with waxed paper.

▪ Bake in a preheated 350°F oven for about 30 minutes, until risen and firm to the touch.

▪ To make the glaze, warm the maple syrup and stir in the buttermilk. Pour this over the warm cake and leave to cool in the pan.

▪ Decorate with whirls of whipped cream and toasted slivered almonds. Alternatively, sprinkle the surface with toasted slivered almonds to cover completely.

Date and orange torte

ACKNOWLEDGMENTS

The publishers would like to thank the following for
their help in the preparation of this volume:

VICKI ROBINSON for the Index

For china, glass and fabrics:

THE DINING ROOM SHOP
White Hart Lane
London SW13

J K HILL
THE HANDMADE POTTERY SHOP
89 Old Brompton Road
London SW7

PERFECT GLASS
5 Park Walk
London SW10

THE REJECT CHINA SHOP
Beauchamp Place
London SW1

JILL SAUNDERS
White Hart Lane
London SW13

TAYLOR & MARR
White Hart Lane
London SW13

WORLD'S END TILES
British Rail Yard
Silverthorne Road
London SW8